HISTRIONICS

Strange Facts About the Great and Famous

Mark Seaman

BUCHAN & ENRIGHT, PUBLISHERS

First published in 1989 by
Buchan & Enright, Publishers (Martins Publishers Limited)
1 Church Road, Shedfield, Southampton, SO3 2HW

British Library Cataloguing in Publication Data

Seaman, Mark
    Histrionics: strange facts about the great
    and famous
    I. Title
    828'.91409

    ISBN 0-907675-85-9

To my Father who, I fancy, might have rather enjoyed reading this.

Photoset in North Wales by
Derek Doyle & Associates, Mold, Clwyd
Printed and bound in Great Britain by
Redwood Burn Limited, Trowbridge, Wiltshire

Contents

Acknowledgements

I would like to express my thanks to my family and friends for their long-standing moral (and practical) support. Special mention should be made of Toby Buchan's perseverance in seeing the project through to publication, in spite of a catalogue of misfortune in its production. Finally, I am indebted to Andrea Thompson, whose superb cover illustration was only excelled by her advice and encouragement.

Mark Seaman, 1989

Illustration Acknowledgements

Page: 2, 39, 41, 73, 82, 89, 95 (main photos), 115, 122, 126 – Hulton; 5, 7, 14 (lower), 25, 31, 42, 45, 53, 60, 94, 98 (Streicher), 102, 116, 128, 133 – courtesy of the Trustees of the Imperial War Museum; 8 (right) – Pinkerton National Detective Agency; 8 (left), 46, 80 – US National Archives; 10, 27, 124 – author; 11 – from an engraving by Horace Vernet; 14 (upper) – King Features; 17 – Stadtmuseum, Munich; 19 – from an engraving by H. Linton; 23 – N.H. Rose Collection of Frontier Photographs; 24 – Señor Pedro Aspé; 29 – *Chicago Tribune*; 30 – the Rt Hon. the Earl Kitchener of Khartoum, TD, DL; 33 – from a photograph by Boissonas & Eggler, St Petersburg; 34 – La Malmaison; 36 – The Rainbird Publishing Group Ltd, from the collection of Sir Owen Morshead; 37 – New York Public Library; 43 – Austrian State Archive-War Archive; 47, 109 – photographs by Matthew Brady, Library of Congress; 50 – Bison Books; 51 – from 'The Defence of Rorke's Drift' by Lady Butler, by gracious permission of Her Majesty the Queen; 58 – Az-Archiv, Vienna; 59 – from 'The Attempt on the Life of Lenin' by P.P. Baloyusov, SCR; 62 – Mercaldo Archive; 63 – N. Ringhart; 65 – Hilscher, Vienna (main photo), Sudd-Verlag (inset); 66 – *L'Illustration*; 70 – *Illustrated London News*; 72 – from the painting by C.E. Fripp, courtesy of the National Army Museum; 75 – Odhams Press; 79 – General Archive of the State Civil Administration, Madrid; 86 – allegory of the French Royal Family (detail), painted in 1670 by Jean Nocret, Musée de Versailles; 87 – Lucca Chml (main photo), Austrian National Library (inset); 88 – Bundesarchiv; 91 – coloured engraving by Gillray; 92 – Heinrich Hoffmann, collection of Al Sherman; 95 (inset) – Viollet; 67 – Library of Congress; 106 – Culver Pictures Inc.; 111 – The Bettmann Archive; 112 – Mansell Collection; 113 – Montana Historical Society; 118 – Mary Evans Picture Library; 119 – Fox Photos; 121 – National Army Museum; 136 – from an engraving by N. Utkin, Russian State Archives.

'Hitler Had Only Got One Stripe'

Adolf Hitler served with distinction in the German Army during the First World War. He served on the Western Front where he was wounded and gassed and, in recognition of his bravery, was awarded the Iron Cross (1st and 2nd Classes). However, the future Führer never rose above the rank of lance-corporal. In contrast, Hermann Goering enjoyed a spectacularly successful war career as an air ace, being credited with having shot down 22 Allied aircraft. Like Hitler, he was wounded and received the Iron Cross, but he was also a celebrated recipient of the famous Pour le Mérite or 'Blue Max'. Although he remained at a relatively junior officer rank, Goering had the distinction of commanding the 'Flying Circus' fighter unit that had been formerly led by the legendary 'Red Baron', Manfred von Richthofen.

Captain Henry Morgan was not only an extremely successful buccaneer, he was also a great survivor. For six years, between 1665 and 1671, he was the Caribbean's most feared pirate, ruthlessly pillaging Spanish trade to such an extent that he crippled that country's interests in the West Indies. But his activities were a source of embarrassment to the local English authorities, so he was arrested and sent back to England. However, the buccaneer showed himself to be as skilful at negotiating his way through the corridors of power as he had been at navigating his way through the reefs of the Spanish Main.

He became popular at court, was favourably received by Charles II and, as a result, was knighted. If that was not enough, the final accolade was bestowed upon him when he was made Lieutenant-Governor of Jamaica. But the leopard had not completely changed his spots. Morgan did not exactly over-extend himself in curbing the activities of his erstwhile colleagues, and in 1683 he was arrested on suspicion of complicity in piracy. Predictably, he survived the charges and, in 1688, was reinstated in office. But he only had a month left to serve; a life of rum and hard living in a harsh climate finally took its toll.

In 1739 England went to war with Spain for reasons of commercial rivalry, but the conflict was not called the 'Anglo-Spanish Trade War'; instead it went by the exotic title of 'The War of Jenkins's Ear'. The pro-war party in London wanted a clash with Spain but lacked a popular

A contemporary cartoon depicts Captain Jenkins displaying his severed ear to a singularly uninterested government minister.

SELF

Special Christmas Rate

$1 AN ISSUE!
12 ISSUES $12

4K21

NAME _____ (PLEASE PRINT)

ADDRESS _____ APT. _____

CITY _____ STATE _____ ZIP _____

☐ Payment enclosed   ☐ Bill me

In Canada, Self is $27 including GST. Your first issue will be mailed within 6 weeks.

ANTOINE VERGLAS

GIFT CERTIFICATE

GIVE A YEAR OF SELF FOR CHRISTMAS

12 ISSUES $12

2K21

To:

NAME
_____
(please print)

ADDRESS _____ Apt. ____

CITY _____ STATE ____ ZIP ____

NAME
_____
(please print)

ADDRESS _____ Apt. ____

CITY _____ STATE ____ ZIP ____

Gift Cards Included

All new subscriptions begin with the January 1992 issue.

MY NAME
_____
(please print)

ADDRESS _____ Apt. ____

CITY _____ STATE ____ ZIP ____

☐ ENTER ☐ RENEW MY OWN SUBSCRIPTION

Total order: _____ gifts @ $12: $ _____

☐ PAYMENT ENCLOSED ☐ BILL ME AFTER 1/1/92

Canada: $27 including GST. Foreign: $27. Offer expires December 31, 1991.

BUSINESS REPLY MAIL

FIRST CLASS PERMIT NO. 365 BOULDER, COLORADO

POSTAGE WILL BE PAID BY ADDRESSEE

SELF

P.O. Box 51988
Boulder, Colorado 80321-1988

NO POSTAGE
NECESSARY
IF MAILED
IN THE
UNITED STATES

motive until they came across one Captain Jenkins, whose ship had been searched by Spanish coastguards in the West Indies. Jenkins had become involved in an altercation with the Spaniards and in the ensuing fracas had had his ear cut off. On his return to England, Jenkins spent his time displaying his aural deprivation (together with his preserved ear as evidence) in the coffee shops of London. Interested politicians and their pamphleteers soon took up the case of the mutilated matelot (who, in truth, was probably only the victim of a bar-room brawl) and demanded vengeance. The result was the War of Jenkins' Ear, that became absorbed into the wider issues of the War of the Austrian Succession – a conflict that was to last for nearly a decade.

Thomas Howard, Duke of Norfolk, stood at Henry VIII's side throughout the many crises of his reign. Whilst others, such as Anne Boleyn, Sir Thomas More, Cardinal Wolsey and Thomas Cromwell, all came and went (usually without their heads), Norfolk survived. In the final years of his life, however, the King developed a persecution mania that was inflamed by his courtiers' obvious concern for their future under a new ruler. In the winter of 1546 Norfolk and his son, the Earl of Surrey, were arrested for treason and sentenced to death. The Earl was executed on 13 January 1547, and his father was to follow him fifteen days later. But on the fourteenth day, the night before Norfolk should have gone to the scaffold, Henry VIII died. The execution was postponed, and for the next six years the Duke was imprisoned in the Tower. In 1553 he was released by Queen Mary and died the next year, a free man. He had lived into his eighties, surviving a remarkably violent era when the life expectancy of a courtier was extremely short.

A portrait of an unusually dandified Congressman Davy Crockett.

The popular image of Davy Crockett is of a man in buckskins, wearing what appears to be a dead animal perched on his head, and invariably fighting Red Indians and alligators. Crockett probably fitted most of this description but he was also a family man, soldier, local politician, Congressman and author. These activities, however, were not the stuff of adventure stories or Hollywood films, and his exploits as a Justice of the Peace and member of Washington committees are generally forgotten. Ironically, his heroic death, which put the finishing touch to the Crockett legend, came about as a result of some important but rather unspectacular events in his life. In 1835 Crockett was approaching his fiftieth year and had recently been widowed for the second time. His defeat in the Congressional elections was the final straw, and he decided to go west on another adventure. His destination was Texas, at the time part of Mexico and struggling for its independence. Crockett joined the fight, but it was to be his last – in 1836 he was killed at the famous battle of the Alamo.

A railway carriage would generally appear to be of little historical interest to anyone but the most enthusiastic of train spotters. But Wagons-Lits car no.2419 was no ordinary piece of rolling stock. In October 1918 it was converted for use by the French commander, Marshal Foch. Later that year, at Compiègne, a group of Germans climbed aboard no.2419 and signed the armistice that ended the First World War. The carriage was now of immense historic significance and was given a place of honour first at the National Army Museum in Paris and later at a specially mounted exhibition at Compiègne. But to millions of Germans, no.2419 was a symbol of Germany's humiliation and it was no coincidence that, in June 1940, Adolf Hitler ordered France's surrender be concluded in the same carriage that witnessed Germany's defeat in 1918. Now no.2419 became a Nazi war trophy and was exhibited in Berlin for several years until Allied

The French delegation about to board carriage No. 2419 and conclude France's surrender, June 1940.

air raids forced its removal to a safer location. By 1945, however, there was nowhere completely safe from Germany's enemies, and the dreadful prospect of a second ignominious surrender loomed. Consequently Hitler ordered that the carriage be destroyed to prevent its falling into Allied hands. An SS unit blew it up, burning everything combustible and even removing all the metalwork. The short but remarkable history of car no.2419 was over.

Peter the Great has been hailed by historians as the man who began the westernisation of Russia and introduced European civilisation to the Slavs. This, however, is not an opinion that would have been shared by the poet John Evelyn. On a visit to England, the Tsar and his uncouth retinue were loaned Evelyn's house at Deptford. Far from displaying culture or sophistication, Peter and his court behaved in a manner that makes a gang of football hooligans look like a Mothers' Union debating society. The lawns were torn up, furniture was broken, the walls were scratched and scraped and Evelyn's paintings were used for target practice. Sir Christopher Wren's estimate for repairing the damage amounted to the then not inconsiderable sum of £350.

Reinhard Heydrich must be in the running for the Third Reich's nastiest Nazi award. He had a hand (and often both hands) in most of the worst excesses of Hitler's Germany, but he had started his adult life as a smart and efficient officer in the German Navy. Perhaps if he had stayed in the service he might have channelled his undeniable organisational powers into more humane directions but, in 1931, he was summarily dismissed from the Navy. The reason was Heydrich's complicated love

Reinhard Heydrich, the philandering naval officer-turned steely-eyed SS-Obergruppenführer.

life. He had become engaged to Lina Mathilde von der Osten, but had then made the double mistake not only of promising to marry another woman, but of choosing a lady with influential friends. When the young naval lieutenant reaffirmed his intention to marry Lina, his spurned lover (who had also learnt of his many other amours) demanded that he be punished for his duplicity. Heydrich was brought before a naval court of honour to defend a charge of ungentlemanly conduct. His attitude towards the court was contemptuous and supercilious, which hardly endeared him to the presiding officer, Admiral Raeder, who just happened to be a family friend of the aggrieved woman. The court ruled that Heydrich was guilty of impropriety and ordered that he be dismissed from the service. Six weeks later the bitter, resentful and unemployed ex-naval officer offered his talents to Heinrich Himmler, the head of a relatively new organisation known as the SS. It was the beginning of his rise to fame and infamy.

Two Kids from the East; the scruffy William Bonney and the elegant Harry Longbaugh – Billy the Kid and the Sundance Kid.

Several of the Wild West's most famous characters were not native-born frontiersmen but originally came from the cities of the eastern seaboard. Billy the Kid, who did most of his killing in the South-West, was probably born in the slums of New York in 1859. He moved west to Kansas when he was three years old before his family finally settled down in New Mexico. A fellow Easterner was Harry Longbaugh, who was better known as Butch Cassidy's partner, the Sundance Kid. While Butch, whose real name was Robert Leroy Parker, was born and bred in the West, the Sundance Kid was brought up in Plainfields, New Jersey.

Quotes

'We taught that goddam horse of yours a lesson.'

This telephone message was communicated by 'Two Gun' Louis Alterie, a member of Chicago's O'Banion gang, during the Prohibition. The horse in question was held responsible for the death of a popular hoodlum, Samuel J. 'Nails' Morton, who had been killed in a riding accident. The grief-stricken gangsters hired the miscreant from the stables, led it to the scene of its misdemeanour and ceremonially executed it, with each member of the gang firing a bullet into the horse's head. The deed done, Alterie informed the stable's owner that revenge had been exacted.

A morose Napoleon contemplates the vicissitudes of family life.

'My family give me no help. They are all insanely ambitious, ruinously extravagant and devoid of talent.'

Napoleon's words merely echo the moans of disgruntled dynasts heard since the first tribe had a chief. But the French emperor had good cause for dissatisfaction, having gone out of his way to keep the fruits of his triumphs in the family, only to find that they became bruised with mishandling. He gave his elder brother, Joseph, the throne of Spain, but he proved to be an abject failure, borrowing money from France when Napoleon intended him to put Spanish gold in the Imperial coffers. Two of his other brothers, Jérôme and Louis, were crowned Kings of Westphalia and Holland respectively, but both were a disappointment. Jérôme was only interested in the easy life of royal pageantry and in his several mistresses, while Louis quarrelled with Napoleon, abdicated and went to Austria. The Emperor's remaining brother, Lucien, also fell out with him. He set off for America but was captured en route by the British, and spent the rest of the Napoleonic Wars in rustic contentment in Worcestershire.

11

Faced with the prospect of entrusting his succession to one of this clan, Napoleon was obliged to undertake the distressing course of divorcing his wife, Josephine, and marrying the daughter of the Emperor of Austria. The marriage took place in April 1810 and, in March the next year, a delighted Napoleon had a son.

'A monster and the greatest villain that ever was born.'

Was George II's comment on the man. His opinion was endorsed by his wife, Queen Caroline, who said, 'If I was to see him in hell, I should feel no more for him than any other rogue who went there.' The object of their disapproval was their own son, Frederick, Prince of Wales. It was common for the Hanoverian monarchs to dislike their heirs, largely because the party opposing the King's government invariably gravitated towards the future ruler. But the hatred felt within the household of George II went far beyond the bounds of the generation gap. The enmity was carried on to the brink of the grave when Caroline, on her deathbed, refused the Prince's request to pay his final respects. Similarly, little paternal grief was displayed when Frederick caught a chill while playing tennis and unexpectedly died a few weeks later, in March 1751.

'Nous sommes dans un pot de chambre et nous y serons emmerdés'

Was the opinion of the French General Auguste Ducrot in September 1870 as he reviewed the parlous situation of his troops facing the Prussian army at Sedan. War had been rashly declared by Napoleon III, and he soon had cause to regret his decision. The French army was surrounded in the 'chamber pot' of Sedan by superior Prussian forces and, as General Ducrot so colourfully put it, they were about to be shat upon. Interestingly, Ducrot's sentiments were echoed by von Moltke, the Prussian Chief of the

General Auguste Ducrot, whose battlefield observation, while distinctly scatological, was nonetheless accurate.

General Staff, who commented, albeit less scatologically, 'Now we have them in a mousetrap.' Nearly 100,000 prisoners were taken by the Prussians, including the Emperor, and the victorious army marched on Paris.

'Nobody shot me.'

This firm denial was made by the Chicago mobster Frank Gusenburg, who had the dubious distinction of being the only victim of the infamous St Valentine's Day Massacre to be still alive when the police arrived on the scene. Bleeding from 14 bullet wounds, Gusenburg was rushed to hospital while detectives pressed him for information as to the identities of his assailants. Gusenburg offered the above statement, adding rather redundantly 'I ain't no copper', and then died.

Some of Frank Gusenberg's fellow victims after the St Valentine's Day Massacre.

Rommel makes a tour of inspection on the Atlantic Wall before his ill-timed spell of home leave.

'It eases my mind to know that while I'm away the tides will be very unfavourable for a landing. Besides, air reconnaissance gives no reason to think it's imminent.'

This parting comment was made by Field-Marshal Erwin Rommel to his naval adviser on 5 June 1944. Germany's celebrated 'Desert Fox' was bidding his staff farewell as he left for a well-deserved leave at home, assuring them that the long-awaited invasion was not about to happen. He was wrong. Later that same night, as Rommel drove homewards, thousands of Allied airborne troops landed in Normandy, followed later the next day by the biggest invasion the world had ever seen.

'By God, sir, I've lost my leg!'
'By God, sir, so you have!'

Lord Uxbridge's exclamation came during a critical moment of the Battle of Waterloo, and perhaps the timing of his injury had something to do with the Duke of Wellington's somewhat casual response. The Duke did, however, catch his cavalry commander as he fell from his horse, his right knee shattered by grapeshot. Almost all of Wellington's staff were wounded during the course of the battle and, by the time he was hit, Lord Uxbridge had had nine horses shot from under him. So there was little surprise that the French aim had finally improved and they had at long last hit the rider, not his mount. But Uxbridge had not passed his last comment of the day. Carried off the field of battle to a hospital tent, Uxbridge was examined by the surgeons. The leg could not be saved, and as the doctors carried out the amputation, Uxbridge only interrupted their work to complain that, in his opinion, the saw did not seem very sharp.

'If I didn't have my hair curled every day I couldn't enjoy my food.'

There was a history of madness in the Bavarian ruling dynasty that reached its peak with King Ludwig II, who was responsible for the above statement. Distinctly odd for most of his twenty-two-year reign, his eccentricity steadily became more pronounced, manifesting itself most obviously in a string of fairy-tale castles and palaces built throughout his alpine kingdom. Having indulged himself with such antics as reversing night and day, inviting his horse to dinner, and providing his palace guard with sofas to stave off fatigue when on duty, Ludwig was finally declared insane and deposed by his uncle. Sadly, the peaceful lunatic was not allowed to live out his days in one of his architectural triumphs. Shortly after a regency had been declared, he was found drowned in a shallow lake. The mystery of his death was further deepened when the corpse of his doctor was fished out of the water shortly afterwards.

'I am not well, get me a glass of brandy.'

One could quite understandably expect this quotation to have been the dying words of an alcoholic, but they are not. In fact, they were uttered by George, Prince of Wales, the eldest son of King George III, in April 1795, upon the occasion of his first meeting with his bride-to-be. Having been coerced into getting married (for reasons of state and relieving his debts), the Prince had made a dreadful choice. His fiancée, Caroline, Princess of Brunswick, was dirty, rarely changed her linen, stank, swore, was eccentric to the point of madness, and was sexually promiscuous (it was rumoured that she had spent the night on deck alone with the first mate of the ship that brought her to England). The only way that the Prince could get through the marriage ceremony was to be in a state of advanced

Ludwig II doffs his hat to reveal a suitably coiffured head, while his fiancée gives the photographer a particularly knowing glance.

King George IV and a misleadingly demure Queen Caroline.

intoxication, which also perhaps explains his consummation of their union on their wedding night. But once was enough. Although the 'happy couple' lived in the same house, they only communicated in writing until they separated a few months later.

'Ce bougre-là a quitté ici avec ses culottes pleines de merde.'

A very free twentieth-century translation of the above might be rendered: 'The little shit has done a runner.' The 'little shit' in question was Napoleon Bonaparte and he had 'run away' from Egypt in August 1799, after an uncharacteristically disastrous campaign in the Middle East. It was the circumstances of his departure that inspired this vitriolic comment from General Kléber, who had only learnt of Napoleon's decision to return to France when he found a note appointing him as the new commander. Kléber's inheritance was a small, sick army, which was seven million francs in debt, and cut off from France by the Royal Navy's blockade. It was to his credit

18

BUONAPARTE AT THE PYRAMIDS.

Napoleon orders his troops to the Pyramids while he promptly beats a hasty retreat back to Paris.

that Kléber made the best of a bad job and was quite successful, until he was assassinated by a Moslem fanatic. His successor, General Menou, was not as able a soldier but had the advantage of being a supreme realist. He became a Moslem and, when all hope of relief from France was at an end, he negotiated terms of surrender with the British that allowed him to take the remnants of his army home.

'Take that you dirty son-of-a-bitch!'

These words, although apparently lifted from a James Cagney movie, were ungratefully spat at a Chicago ambulanceman by Mike 'The Devil' Genna, a notorious mobster. Dying from a severed artery after being wounded during a gunfight, Genna was laid on a stretcher. Then, summoning up his last dregs of energy, he uttered the above comment, and kicked the unfortunate medic in the face. It was to be his last act on earth as he promptly fell back and died.

'I tell you that Wellington is a bad general, that the English are bad troops and that this is going to be a picnic.'

Perhaps it is just that the more famous a man becomes, the more people record what he says. This may explain why Napoleon seems to have been so prone to making ill-advised comments such as the above quote. Speaking to Marshal Soult on the morning of the Battle of Waterloo, Napoleon rejected his Chief of Staff's recommendation that he be cautious. The Emperor, never having met Wellington in battle, told Soult, 'Just because Wellington has beaten you, you think he is a great general.' By the end of the day, Napoleon had been forced to revise his opinion.

'How amused the servants would be to find us in bed together'

Was the naive wedding-night comment of the Grand Duke Peter to his young bride. In fact, Peter was more than just an innocent, being somewhat retarded, both physically and mentally. While her husband contented himself by playing with toy soliders, his highly sexed wife, the future Catherine the Great, grew ever more frustrated. The unhappy couple probably remained virgins for the next seven years until Catherine took a lover and Peter had an operation carried out on his genitals. The results were immediate, if confusing: Catherine had a miscarriage and her husband took a mistress. Although Peter's rehabilitation was such that the two occasionally slept together, it is probable that he remained sterile and that the child born to Catherine in 1754 was fathered by her lover, Saltykov.

'I've done my report. It consists of three words – "There aren't any."'

Colonel Roly Sword's taciturn exposition of Poland's defences against invasion was not only a masterpiece of brevity but was profoundly prophetic. Within months of the British Military Attaché in Warsaw making this assessment, in September 1939, Poland was overrun by Hitler's panzers and Stalin's Red Army.

German soldiers make heavy weather of removing a frontier barrier in contrast to the ease with which they overran the Polish defences.

21

Madness and Eccentricity

In the days of the American Wild West, justice was usually defined as being on the side of the man who could shoot fastest. But inevitably, civilisation began to reach the frontier and a facade of a legal system appeared. Probably the most colourful exponent of the cowboy judiciary was Judge Roy Bean who, in 1882, was appointed Justice of the Peace for the Texas town of Vinegaroon. Bean's knowledge of the law was, to put it mildly, rudimentary, his qualifications being ownership of a law book and a long personal experience of being on the receiving end of law courts. In fact, Vinegaroon soon died as quickly as it had sprung up, and Bean moved on to the township of Langtry. Here, the Judge was to hold court for the next two decades, working out of his saloon, the 'Jersey Lilly' (*sic*). His rulings were characterised by their arbitrary nature and minimal relationship to the law. Thus the killer of a Chinaman was acquitted because Bean was unable to locate any specific mention of the act as a felony in his law book. Another murderer was freed because Bean ruled that it was the victim's fault for getting in front of the gun. Even dead men were still liable for punishment. The judge penalised a corpse who had left a revolver and $40; the cadaver was charged with illegally 'carrying' a weapon and was fined the sum of $40.

The Emperor Caligula was well received by the people of Rome when he succeeded the dissipated Tiberius, but they

The idiosyncratic Judge Roy Bean and his saloon/court house

soon changed their minds. At first Caligula's odd behaviour only affected the Imperial court, who became the victims of his whims and insane plans. Senators had to behave like slaves and trot alongside Caligula's chariot, relatives who might be potential rivals for the throne were ordered to commit suicide, and brides at society weddings ran the risk of being abducted in the middle of the ceremony if the Emperor took a fancy to them. Caligula managed to possess just about all the character disorders in the psychiatrist's textbook, revelling in his power and indulging his sadism with comments to his executioner such as 'Strike him so that he feels he is dying.' And the mad emperor did not confine himself to projects solely within the palace walls; Caligula delighted in schemes whose only justification was perversity. Thus harbours were constructed at places where the sea was at its deepest, tunnels were mined through solid rock, mountains were flattened, and plains were transformed into mountains. This lunacy was tolerated for four years, before the Emperor was assassinated by his bodyguard, whose actions for once reflected popular sentiment.

It has been claimed that it was the deaths of Jonathan Swift's two mistresses in 1723 and 1728 that put him on the road to madness. He suffered increasingly acute attacks of vertigo, and his sanity disintegrated with old age until, in 1742, guardians were appointed to look after his person and affairs. By the time of his death three years later, the author of *Gulliver's Travels* was in a world as remote and fantastic as the one that he had invented for his classic novel.

Charlotte, Empress of Mexico, became unbalanced after her husband, Maximilian, was executed in 1867. On her return to Europe, she developed a persecution mania, being convinced that an Italian street organ-grinder was a

The Empress Charlotte in mourning.

colonel in the Mexican espionage network that had been set up to ensnare her. Arriving in Rome, she was certain that assassins were plotting her death, poisoning her food, her drink, and even her combs. As a result, she only drank from the Trevi Fountains because she knew that her persecutors could not tamper with this water. In desperation she sought refuge with the Pope, forcing an entry into the Vatican and then refusing to leave. She snatched the Pope's drinking chocolate from his hands and successfully demanded to be allowed to stay the night, thereby creating an extremely awkward dilemma for Papal protocol.

General Erich Ludendorff took as his second wife a doctor who specialised in mental diseases, but she appears to have been unable to do anything to arrest the progress of her husband's increasingly eccentric behaviour. He had been

General Ludendorff – an imposing glower masks an eccentric and gullible personality.

an extremely successful general in the early stages of the First World War and, towards the end, had wielded immense political power. Perhaps Ludendorff felt himself to be in some measure responsible for Germany's disastrous post-war economic depression, which was worsened by a mammoth £6,600,000,000 reparations bill payable to the Allies. In an attempt to expiate his guilt, Ludendorff resolved to pay this debt himself. He contacted a man called Tausend who, it was rumoured, possessed a magic box that produced paper money. At great expense Ludendorff managed to buy the box – but the only money he saw was the cash he paid to Tausend.

King George III, who reigned from 1760 to 1820, was for lengthy periods quite mad. Historians have detected the first signs of insanity as early as 1765, but it was in October 1788 that the 'flying gout' truly took a grip. The King's physical condition deteriorated, he developed insomnia and suffered acute delirium that made him talk rapidly and incessantly. And his state of mind was scarcely helped by the barbaric medical 'treatment' to which he was subjected. Amongst the so-called remedies were irritants applied to his legs to draw away the 'humours', but which merely served to hurt him, prevent sleep and increase irritability. Understandably, the King removed them and, for his pains, was put in a strait-jacket by his doctors. Although the King made a recovery, it was by no means permanent and he suffered recurrent relapses as he grew older. For the last years of his life, George spent most of his time wandering in the gardens of his palaces, blind, deaf and talking to the trees.

The boy-emperor Elagabalus ranks high in the list of insane Roman rulers. Only fourteen years old when he

A coin showing the prematurely aged features of the Emperor Elagabalus.

came to the throne in 218 AD, he indulged virtually every whim, vice and excess known to man (or boy), using the full resources of the empire to achieve them. His appointments on becoming emperor were eccentric in the extreme: a ballet dancer became Prefect of the Guard, a charioteer was made the Commander of the Watch, and the Imperial barber took over the supervision of Rome's grain supplies. Bisexual and totally given up to hedonism, Elagabalus was constantly taking perfumed baths and once showered his guests with an avalanche of sweet-smelling flower petals (it did not seem to matter too much that this inundation caused some unfortunates to be smothered to death). No matter how difficult or expensive his demands, they were carried out. When he wished to see a mountain of snow, buckets of the stuff were fetched and piled high before him. A ton of spiders' webs was collected to appease his curiosity, and a meal of six hundred storks' heads (he only ate the brains) satisfied his appetite. After four years, Elagabalus was deposed, his end forming a stark contrast with the luxury and indulgence of his reign. His mutinous guard found him hiding in a lavatory, killed him on the spot, and then threw his headless corpse into the Tiber.

27

Field-Marshal Prince von Blücher was Prussia's leading general during the Napoleonic wars, his greatest victory being achieved as commander of his country's troops at the Battle of Waterloo. He was somewhat mentally unbalanced and was very fond of a tipple, which had the combined effect of making him prone to bouts of insanity and eccentric behaviour. In 1809 he became convinced that he was pregnant as a result of having been raped by a French soldier. His lunatic fantasy was completed by his conviction that his offspring would be an elephant. This French connection continued into his persecution mania. He believed Napoleon's agents lit fires under the floorboards of his quarters so that they were too hot to walk upon. His solution to this problem was to cross the room by leaping from one piece of furniture to another.

During the Prohibition era in Chicago, the man dominating City Hall was Mayor William 'Big Bill' Thompson, the major characteristics of whose administration were graft and corruption, set against a background of unrelenting gang warfare. Naturally enough, 'Big Bill's' record in office was not the prominent feature of his re-election campaign, especially as he had managed to transform a $3 million surplus into a $4.5 million deficit in four years, and law-and-order was definitely not a subject for debate. Instead, Thompson mounted a vehement attack upon Great Britain and its monarchy, hoping to swing the support of anglophobic immigrant workers and deflect criticism of the mayhem raging in the streets. While tommy guns spat bullets and bootleggers reigned supreme, Thompson was pledging to 'punch King George in the snoot' if he ever came to the city, and claimed, 'If King George had his way, there'd be a million American boys in China today to fight the battle for the dirty

William 'Big Bill' Thompson, Mayor of Chicago, anti-monarchist, and rabid anglophobe.

Englishman and help the King make a billion dollars in the opium trade.' At a time when local newspapers were shackled by the mobsters who dictated what news was printed, the Mayor revealed a 'conspiracy to destroy American history on behalf of the King of England'. Of course, in the topsy-turvy world that was Chicago in the 1920s, 'Big Bill' was re-elected. But there was some justice in the end: Thompson invited 1,500 campaign workers to a victory party on his yacht, but the weight of illegal booze and roisterous revellers was too much and the boat sank at its moorings.

The famous soldier and statesman, Lord Kitchener, was a very straitlaced person, perhaps as a result of his father's eccentricity. Kitchener senior, a former army officer, held many strange opinions on a host of subjects, including a distrust of schools, which rendered his son virtually

Lieutenant-Colonel Kitchener, the father of the somewhat more famous Field-Marshal.

illiterate until his early teens. His oddest theory was that blankets were unhealthy and should be replaced as bedclothes by old newspapers, which he considered were cheap, clean and just as effective. He therefore had sheets of *The Times* sewn together and hung across his bed, suspending them from boards constructed around the bedframe. Initially he had wanted to sleep wrapped in paper but Mrs Kitchener complained that the rustling would keep her awake at night. Mr Kitchener would surely have been forgiven if he had replied that at least he had furnished her with something to read during her bouts of insomnia.

Gustav Krupp von Bohlen und Halbach was a very well ordered and self-disciplined man. He needed to be, for on marrying the heiress to the massive Krupp industrial empire, he took on the mantle of Germany's most powerful businessman. Gustav's life was lived to a precise timetable, with each meal beginning and ending at a specified time, and bedtime coming always at precisely 10.15 pm – perhaps this regularity assisted Gustav in the fathering of a thriving Krupp dynasty of eight children. This strict regimentation was carried into his leisure activities. One of his hobbies was the scrutinisation of railway timetables, looking for typographical errors, savouring a mistake, and telephoning the railway to castigate them for their inaccuracy.

Lord Raglan (left) confers with his Turkish and French allies.

Major-General Fitzroy James Henry Somerset, Lord Raglan, was the commander of the British Expeditionary Force to the Crimea in 1854. It was his first command of an army in the field and, at the age of sixty-five, he was well past it. Nevertheless, he was a kind old boy and his staff liked him, although his forgetfulness caused several problems. In spite of the fact that the Napoleonic wars had been over for nearly forty years and the French were now Britain's allies, Raglan had an unfortunate tendency to talk of the 'French' at staff meetings whenever he meant the 'enemy'.

Q. What is the similarity between Marshal Blücher and the Empress Alexandra of Russia?
A. They both suffered from phantom pregnancies.
Although Blücher's condition was brought on by excess of alcohol and mental instability, the Tsarina was the victim of a quack doctor's administrations. During a visit to France she had been introduced to 'Doctor' Philippe Nizier-Vachot, a faith healer and mystic who claimed that his magical powers could ensure that the Tsarina would give birth to a male heir. Such was his ability to impose auto-suggestion that Alexandra went into a phantom pregnancy, displaying all the signs of approaching motherhood, including a swollen stomach. Eventually, more conventional medical opinion was sought and confirmed that she was not going to have a baby. Amidst considerable royal embarrassment, 'Doctor' Philippe was sent back to France. There seems little doubt that the Imperial Family were aware of Nizier-Vachot's lack of credentials as they had arranged for special dispensation in order that he could practise in Russia. However, they may not have known that 'Doctor' Philippe was a former Lyons butcher's assistant who had a number of convictions in France for practising medicine without a licence.

The Empress Alexandra showing few signs of any real or imaginary pregnancy.

Whatever Became of ...?

An all-too-brief moment of affectionate repose shared by Napoleon and his son.

Napoleon spent nearly a decade trying to secure his dynasty until, in March 1811, to his unconfined joy, his wife gave birth to a son. But an heir is never an automatic guarantee that an empire will endure, and four years later Napoleon was defeated at Waterloo and sent into exile on St Helena. But what of his son? Obviously, Napoleon's former enemies feared that the child would become the focal point for dissidents loyal to his father, but the situation was complicated by the fact that the boy's mother was the Austrian Emperor's daughter. Napoleon's son was therefore brought up at the Habsburg court in Vienna, given the title of Franz, Duke of Reichstadt, and closely observed for any sign of malcontent. When a European throne became vacant, Reichstadt's name was usually mentioned but was always rejected. Circumstances were, however, to preclude his ever being seriously considered, for he contracted tuberculosis and, after 1831, his health was most delicate. Finally, amidst great sadness at court – for Reichstadt was a most personable young man – he died on 22 July 1832. But more than a century after his death, Reichstadt again became a political pawn. In an attempt to cement emotional ties between defeated France and Nazi Germany, the Duke's remains were removed from the Capuchin Church in Vienna and in December 1940 were reinterred next to those of his father in Les Invalides in Paris.

Like many fashion setters, Beau Brummell's rise was meteoric and his fall profound. While affecting lowly origins, George Bryan Brummell had been to Eton and Oxford and, although not of the aristocracy, his charm, wit and, above all, elegance made him the leader of London's young society in the 1800s. But after a decade as the close friend of the Prince of Wales and leading a lifestyle of unrelenting extravagance, Brummell had burnt himself out. He fell out with his royal disciple and slipped so heavily into debt that, in 1816, he fled to France in order to escape his creditors. His decline continued and he was finally imprisoned for his debts, this time run up in Normandy. Now in his fifties and far from the handsome Regency buck of yesteryear, his health gave way. In 1837 he was committed to a lunatic asylum at Caen and died there in March 1840

Beau Brummell at the height of his fame.

The outlaw and sometime race-track worker, Frank James.

In contrast to his brother Jesse's violent end, Frank James lived to a ripe old age, dying peacefully at the family ranch in Missouri in February 1915. After Jesse's murder in April 1882, Frank surrendered to the authorities and was soon standing trial (in an opera house) for a double slaying. Acquitted in 1883, he joined a Wild West show before finally ending his working life as a starter at a horse-race track. If anything, Frank appears to have been something of a bore, with a penchant for quoting Shakespeare and the Bible that so annoyed the other members of the gang that on one occasion Jesse was moved to turn on him with a gun.

It is common knowledge that H.M. Stanley found David Livingstone in the heart of the African jungle, introducing himself with the famous presumption. But having made contact once more with the outside world, what happened to Livingstone? The reason for his apparent relapse into obscurity is simple: Livingstone had completed virtually all his major explorations and his ruined health prevented him from undertaking any more really taxing expeditions. He did spend several months exploring with Stanley after their meeting in November 1871, but a renewed attack of dysentery early in 1873 forced him to curtail his travels. The missionary-explorer died in Africa in May 1873, aged sixty, appropriately kneeling in prayer at the side of his bed.

Most people's knowledge of William Bligh ends when he was dumped in a small boat by the *Bounty's* mutineers and told to find his own way home. But although Bligh was tactless, harsh and severe, he was a superb sailor and

Captain William Bligh, renowned sailor and notorious disciplinarian.

managed to sail his boat (together with a crew of loyal seamen) some 4,000 miles to safety. Contrary to expectations, his career did not unduly suffer from the loss of the *Bounty*. But lightning was to strike twice more. In 1797 Bligh's new command, HMS *Director*, mutinied. Once again, he bounced back, and was appointed Governor of New South Wales. Sadly, his well-known character traits led to a particularly stormy period in office, and he found himself confronted by a third mutiny arising from his 'oppressive behaviour'. But the Admiralty still saw his disciplinarian attitude as an asset rather than a liability, and Bligh had attained the elevated rank of Vice-Admiral before his death in 1817, aged sixty-three.

The Charge of the Light Brigade is one of the most celebrated cavalry actions of history, but few of the participants lived to tell the tale of their heroism. Out of

The epitome of the Victorian, aristocratic military commander, the Earl of Cardigan.

about 700 men (not Tennyson's 'noble six hundred') only 195 returned from the 'Valley of Death'. The commander of the Light Brigade, Lord Cardigan, was one of the lucky survivors who, to give him credit, had led his men from the front and personally reached the Russian guns. But that is as far as one can go in praising him. Whilst the battered remnants of his command faced two more years of fighting, within a couple of months Cardigan was sailing home aboard his yacht. In England he was hailed as a hero by the press and populace and, to cap it all, was invited to Windsor Castle to tell the Royal Family of his feats of derring-do. It was only a couple of years later, when the veterans returned, that Cardigan's image began to suffer. Admittedly he had reached the Russian guns, but he had not wasted much time leaving them, and his culpability in leading the charge up the wrong valley gradually became known. For the rest of his life he was by turns hailed as a hero and vilified as an aristocratic braggart. To make matters worse, in 1858 he contracted a dubious marriage, with an eccentric young woman half his age, which was to leave him a pariah. His last years were spent in worsening health that was matched by his fading bank balance. He died in March 1868, having suffered a stroke whilst out riding.

Throughout the First World War, Kaiser Wilhelm II was labelled a blood-crazed monster by the Allied press. All manner of bestial crimes were laid at his door, and a campaign was launched to ensure his execution after the eventual Allied triumph. But strangely, in spite of all the recriminations and angry words, the Kaiser never became involved in a war crimes trial. He abdicated his throne in November 1918 to allow peace negotiations to progress more easily, and slipped across the border into neutral Holland. He was to live there in relative peace and tranquillity for more than twenty years, settling down on a modest estate near Doorn. He momentarily became a

Kaiser Wilhelm II in old age with his second wife, Hermione. His first wife died in April 1921, expressing a deathbed request that her husband remarry. Wilhelm certainly took her at her word, and married Hermione, Princess of Schoenaich-Carolath-Beuthen, the following year.

figure of some importance once again in 1940, following the Nazi invasion of the Netherlands, when he refused both the British offer of asylum in the United Kingdom and a similar offer from Hitler that he return to Germany. He died in 1941, aged eighty-two.

The lady with the lamp is one of the best-known images of Victorian England, second only to the Queen herself. Florence Nightingale's work during the Crimean War helped to foster the development of military medicine and professional nursing and, more than a century later, earned her a distinguished place on the back of a ten-pound note. After the war, her career was dominated by her campaigns for medical reform throughout the Empire. She never married, and led a highly active life until her mid-seventies when she took to her bedroom for good. Her sight had troubled her since 1867 and, by the

The lady without her lamp – Florence Nightingale.

late 1880s, she was virtually blind, while her mind also began to fail. For the last four years of her life she was all but comatose, experiencing ever-lengthening periods of unconsciousness. Finally in August 1910, the farce ended and she passed away at the not inconsiderable age of ninety years and three months.

The assassination of the Archduke Franz Ferdinand at Sarajevo in June 1914 was the flashpoint that led to the outbreak of the First World War. Naturally enough, the world's attention was diverted away from the small Balkan town and the fate of the assassins. Gavrilo Princip, the man who fired the shots, and twenty-four of his fellow conspirators were arrested and put on trial. Sixteen were found guilty, of whom three were executed. Princip and several others, however, were still juveniles and, as a result, were spared the death penalty. Princip and two

The men who sparked off the First World War sitting in the court-room at Sarajevo.

others died of tuberculosis in prison during the war that they had helped to begin. Two of the conspirators who were released after the war ironically pursued careers that gave them ample opportunity to reflect upon their roles in history: one became Professor of History at Belgrade University, and the other later held the post of Curator at Sarajevo's museum.

'Your Country needs you!' was the exhortation that made Lord Kitchener famous and, for most of his life, his country certainly needed him. He was the nation's foremost soldier for nearly two decades, earning himself a reputation in the Sudan and South Africa as the man who could always be relied upon to put matters right. He was therefore a popular choice as Secretary of State for War on the outbreak of the First World War in August 1914. As the conflict soon showed itself to be a marathon rather than a sprint, Kitchener set about organising new, massed armies to fight the slogging match on the Western Front. But while his reputation with the public and rank-and-file remained as high as ever, his relations with his fellow senior officers and politicians had, by 1916, greatly deteriorated. However, in June that year all political rivalry was ended when Kitchener was drowned off the Orkneys, after the warship in which he was sailing to Russia was sunk by a German mine.

In 1881 Pat Garrett shot and killed Billy the Kid. It brought the lawman instant fame but little else. He had to take legal action to get his reward money and lost his job as sheriff. There followed a period of travel throughout the South-West, working on ranches, in law enforcement, and even as a collector of customs at El Paso (a job arranged for him by President Theodore Roosevelt). Finally, in 1908,

Field-Marshal Kitchener, revealing an eye cast that was not evident in his famous recruiting poster.

Pat Garrett, the celebrated killer of Billy the Kid.

Garrett's colourful life was brought to an abrupt close. He got into an argument with Wayne Brazil, a tenant who was ranching his land for him, and in the ensuing fracas Garrett was shot in the head and stomach. Brazil was, nevertheless, able to enter a successful plea of self-defence when sent to trial.

Following his success in the American Civil War, General Ulysses Simpson Grant stayed at the forefront of his country's affairs for more than a decade. When the war finished he became Seceretary of State for War and, in 1868, began the first of his two terms as President of the United States. Sadly, Grant was no politician and the next eight years were dominated by economic depression, monetary scandals and governmental corruption. He retired from politics in 1877 and devoted himself to a business career that was, if anything, even more

A despondent President Grant fails to raise a smile for the camera.

calamitous than his Presidency. Grant had become heavily involved in the founding of a banking house, so when this went bankrupt in 1884, his personal finances were ruined. Sick, poor and having lost everything, Grant set about writing his memoirs to provide a future source of income for his wife. With the help of Mark Twain as his publisher, Grant won his last battle and, after his death from cancer of the throat in 1885, his widow was left financially secure.

Illness

Princess Alexandra models her famous choker.

Princess Alexandra, the wife of Edward, Prince of Wales, was beautiful and popular, thereby ensuring that she would become a trendsetter in dress and style. It was odd, therefore, that illness determined two of her most famous gifts to Victorian high society. She covered an unsightly mark on her neck (caused by a cold-sore) with a jewelled choker that was quickly affected by her blemish-free admirers. A much stranger fashion was the 'Alexandra Limp', which ladies took up in imitation of the Princess's unusual walk. However, this was no regal affectation but a genuine handicap, being the legacy of a bout of rheumatic fever.

Jean-Paul Marat, the French Revolutionary leader, was noted for his irritability. What his contemporaries did not realise was that the bad-tempered politician was suffering from pruritus and pityriasis simplex: two skin diseases whose symptoms of incessant itching were hardly conducive to a tranquil frame of mind. In the event, this illness was indirectly to prove fatal, for it was whilst taking one of his frequent baths, which served to reduce the irritation, that Charlotte Corday ended his discomfort – permanently – by stabbing him to death on 13 July 1793.

In the spring of 1945, the Allied armies were advancing into Germany and Hitler's Reich was falling apart. But then, so too was Hitler. A chronic hypochondriac, he suffered from gastric pains, flatulence, severe stomach cramps, a swollen abdomen, kidney pains and insomnia. Not unnaturally, he was moved to place great faith in his personal physician, Dr Theodor Morell. However, his opinion was not universally endorsed, for many felt that Morell was a quack, and Goering labelled him 'Reich Injection Master' because of the vast quantities of drugs that he pumped into Hitler's veins. At one time the Führer was receiving twenty-eight different types of medication, including 'Multiflor' capsules (containing intestinal bacteria from Bulgarian cattle), and injections of biologicals from bulls' testicles.

A distinctly haggard Adolf Hitler, as he looked at the beginning of 1945.

All sorts of reasons have been given for the fall of the Romanov dynasty, from the Tsar's decision to enter the First World War to the haemophilia of his son. Many, however, ascribe the rise of Rasputin as the main cause of the Imperial downfall and, if this is the case, it was a sick dog that started the rot, not the Tsarevitch. For Rasputin's entrée into court circles came about after he had successfully cured the ailing pet dog of the Grand Duke Nicholas.

Lieutenant Gonville Bromhead was deaf. He was also thirty-three years old in 1879, and had been in the British Army for twelve years. Coming from an established soldiering family, his prospects for rapid promotion had

An artist's impression of the Defence of Rorke's Drift, with Bromhead struggling to hear his comrade's orders over the din of battle.

looked good, but, with the onset of his disability, his career ground to a halt. In the 1870s there was no effective hearing-aid available so he had to soldier on in silence, inevitably to the confusion and annoyance of his men. His superiors tried to give Bromhead and his company tasks that would not tax or expose his handicap, with the result that they were usually employed on dull or tiring duties. It was on one such onerous task, during the Zulu War of 1879, that Bromhead and his men found themselves stationed at Rorke's Drift, guarding a supply dump and river crossing. Thus, thanks in no small part to the Lieutenant's deafness, they were to participate in one of the British Army's most glorious actions and Bromhead was to win the Victoria Cross.

Kaiser Wilhelm II went to great lengths to personify the Prussian war-lord. He was rarely photographed out of uniform, always unsmiling and usually striking a pose of disdainful resolution. But the image was flawed. Much of the Kaiser's posturing was specifically intended to disguise the fact that his left arm was crippled. Thus all the martial stances, with his hand resting on his sword hilt or clasping a field-marshal's baton to his side, were designed to hide his disability. It is thought that Wilhelm's arm had been pulled out of its socket at birth and, in spite of the countless royal servants in attendance, nothing was done at the time to remedy the condition. By the time corrective steps were taken it was too late. Electric treatment on the deformed arm merely hurt the patient, adding one more neurosis to a person who was to build up an impressive collection by his maturity.

Towards the end of his reign Henry VIII was a physical wreck. In his youth he had been an athlete possessed of

Kaiser Wilhelm's deformed left hand is kept in the shadows, unobtrusively resting on his sword hilt.

great stamina and strength, but his later years were marred by debilitating illness that increased his mega-lomania. Years of overeating and too much drinking had made him obese, while an indiscriminate sex life had resulted in venereal disease. He suffered from dropsy and persistent ulcers on his legs that, on occasion, made him quite speechless with pain. If this was not enough, it seems likely that a glandular condition contributed to his general malaise. But Henry's medical history was not without its successes: he did at least avoid the Tudors' susceptibility to tuberculosis, which claimed his father, brother and two of his own sons.

In late 1871, the Prince of Wales fell dangerously ill with typhoid fever, the very sickness that had killed his father, Prince Albert. But there the similarity ends, for, while the father tried to fight off the illness constantly attended by his loving wife, Queen Victoria, the son's wife was often barred from the sick room. The reason for Princess Alexandra's exclusion, by order of Victoria and the doctors, had nothing to do with any concern over her own health but rather that the Prince, in his fever, was talking in great detail of his numerous sexual escapades. After a period of crisis, the Prince pulled through, his recovery marked by a request for a bottle of Bass beer, revealing another stark contrast to the character of his father.

Assassinations and Murders

Nero's love life was more than a little bit complicated, but he had in his power the means to simplify it – murder. Although he had a wife and many mistresses, the dominant woman in Nero's life was his mother, Agrippina, who had ruthlessly masterminded her son's path to the Imperial throne. But steadily, as his self-confidence grew, Nero became less dependent upon Agrippina. Independence changed to antagonism when he decided that he wanted to divorce his wife and marry his mistress, Poppaea Sabina. Agrippina refused to sanction the change in her son's domestic arrangements, so Nero resolved to kill his mother. As an old hand at administering poison, Agrippina was too wily to be killed off by that method. Nero therefore lured her on to a ship and then had it sunk; Agrippina, however, survived the shipwreck and managed to swim ashore. Now subtlety was dispensed with, and a gang of assassins raided Agrippina's villa and stabbed her to death. There only remained Nero's wife, Octavia, as an impediment to the realisation of her husband's plans, but she proved as stubborn as her mother-in-law had been. Nero's answer was to sentence her to death on trumped-up charges of infidelity, and although his men were unable to bleed Octavia to death, they asphyxiated her in a steambath. But marriage to Poppaea was, in the end, not all sweetness and light. One day, in a fit of rage, Nero kicked his pregnant wife in the stomach and killed her.

The twentieth century has no monopoly of revolutions
and assassination plots. Even in the supposed calm and
stability of Georgian England an ambitious plot was laid to
overthrow the monarchy and government. Led by Arthur
Thistlewood, the illegitimate son of a Lincolnshire farmer,
a conspiracy was formed to dethrone George IV and
proclaim a republic. The first step was to be the murder of
the entire Cabinet who, propitiously, were scheduled to
dine together on 23 February 1820 at Lord Harrowby's
house in Grosvenor Square. Having disposed of the
government in one fell swoop, the conspirators anticipated
little problem in seizing control of London. While the plan
for widespread revolution was hare-brained, the assassination plot was quite practical. But as is frequently the
case, the conspirators' security was non-existent and the
authorities soon knew of their intentions. Lord Harrowby's dinner party was cancelled and a force of police and

The shoot-out in Cato Street between the conspirators and the forces of law and order.

soldiers raided the revolutionaries' hideout in Cato Street, off the Edgware Road. A violent and confused affray ensued, during which Thistlewood killed a constable before making his escape with several of the gang. He was, however, captured the next day and, with the wheels of justice running abnormally fast, was hanged outside Newgate Gaol in May 1820

The early Tsars had a tendency to test the adage that blood is thicker than water. Ivan the Terrible killed his eldest son in a fit of anger, but Peter the Great was far more calculating in the murder of his son, the Tsarevitch Alexis. For a host of real and imagined reasons, father and son were totally incompatible. Alexis feared Peter's rages (so much so that on one occasion he tried to shoot himself, but only succeeded in burning his hand); Peter, for his part, was disappointed in his son's weak character, but also recognised that Alexis was a potential focus for rebellion. After years of threats, recriminations and sporadic reconciliations, Alexis ran away to Austria in 1716. He was only away for a year and a half, Peter having promised to forgive and forget and, more significantly, having put pressure on the Austrian Emperor to send Alexis back to Russia. The Tsarevitch enjoyed five months of precarious freedom in St Petersburg before he was confined in the Fortress of Peter and Paul. Whilst an assembly of nobles and clergy pondered over his fate, the matter was taken out of their hands: Alexis died while undergoing torture. The means of death was the knout, a whip made of parchment, hardened with milk, that was so heavy and sharp that three blows could kill. It is recorded that Alexis managed to endure twenty-five strokes in one day, but no-one could long withstand the dreadful beating, which, possibly, was administered by his father. Although it was common knowledge how Alexis had died, an official communiqué delicately stated that he had succumbed to 'a cruel disease resembling apoplexy'.

On 30 June 1934 Hitler carried out a purge of the Nazi Party, eliminating dissidents and disposing of embarrassments. His main target was the SA, a paramilitary force that he now saw as a threat to his own authority. Its leader, Ernst Röhm, was arrested and generously given the opportunity to take his own life. After ten minutes of sitting in his cell with a loaded pistol, SS guards went in and helped Röhm out, shooting him three times in the chest and head. In the course of the purge, known as the 'Night of the Long Knives', others were not to be treated so respectfully: SA Obergruppenfuehrer Heines was arrested when in bed with a young man and, along with other senior SA men, was put up against a wall and shot. Old scores were settled, such as when the man who had defeated Hitler's 1923 Putsch was beaten to death and his body dumped on a heath. In the mayhem mistakes were inevitably made and Willi Schmid, the music critic, received the bullets intended for Willi Schmidt. But perhaps the most poignant episode of the purge involved

Goering, one of the masterminds behind the Night of the Long Knives, with two of his victims; the bridegroom Ernst and the wedding guest Rohm.

Karl Ernst, one of Röhm's most trusted confederates. Ernst had just got married and was about to begin his honeymoon with a sea cruise when the SS caught up with him. Instead of a voyage on a luxury liner, Ernst went on a one-way trip to Berlin.

Soviet historians tend to paint a picture of Lenin as the benign, universally loved father figure of modern Russia, conveniently forgetting his many political enemies. In August 1918 he was shot and badly wounded, but so great was the fear of another assassination attempt that his followers would not take him to a hospital, preferring to treat him in the security of his own apartment. The attack had been carried out by Dora Kaplan, a twenty-eight-year-old Social Revolutionary, who considered Lenin to be a 'traitor to the revolution'. Walking to his car after addressing a meeting of workers, Lenin was accosted by

An artist's impression of the attempted assassination of Lenin. The victim looks as if he has slipped on the snow or succumbed to a surfeit of vodka.

Kaplan on the pavement and was hit by two bullets at point-blank range. One lodged in his left shoulder, whilst the other pierced the left-hand side of his neck and, travelling through his body, ended up near his right collar bone. In spite of extremely cavalier medical treatment, which resulted in the bullets remaining in his body, Lenin survived. Kaplan was not so fortunate. Attempts to make her name accomplices failed and she was executed by Malkov, the commandant of the Kremlin, a couple of days after the incident.

There was usually a lack of subtlety about the way in which the Nazis disposed of their enemies. In the days of the street battles with the Communists it was boots and clubs, but with the seizure of power came the detached automation of the concentration camps. In 1943, however, they dreamed up something a bit special for King Boris III

Boris III's successor, the Regent, Prince Cyrill, still wearing an armband in honour of his dead brother, understandably casts a wary eye around Hitler's headquarters in December 1943.

of Bulgaria. In August Hitler summoned him to Berlin for talks, in the hope of checking Boris's increasingly anti-German stance. The conference did not solve the problem, but the flight home did, for shortly after his return to Sofia, Boris died. The cause of death was given out as heart failure, but it seems probable that German agents were responsible. The King's brother, Prince Cyril, believed that too rich an oxygen mix had been fed into the royal face-mask, while another theory claimed that Boris's mask was faulty and the Geman pilot flew the aircraft deliberately high. Less inventive but probably more correct is the conclusion that Boris had been given some form of slow-acting poison during his visit. His subsequent demise on Bulgarian soil from ostensibly natural causes could therefore conveniently direct suspicion away from his German enemies.

James Butler Hickok, better known as 'Wild Bill Hickok', was one of the Wild West's most deadly gunmen. By 1876, though, he was slowing down (he had been born in 1837) and, not unnaturally, it worried him. The man who had driven stagecoaches, fought in the Civil War and against the Indians, later tried his hand at starring in a Wild West Show, but he did not like the life and went west again. He made his way to Deadwood City, South Dakota, troubled by failing eyesight and having suffered, three years earlier, the distressing experience of reading his own obituary published in the *Missouri Democrat*. On 2 August 1876 he was sitting in Carl Mann's saloon playing poker with some friends when Jack McCall walked in and shot him in the head. There seemed little reason for the murder, though it has been alleged that McCall was a hired assassin. The alternative explanation is that the murderer had lost to Hickok at poker earlier that day and was probably drunk when he exacted his revenge. Usually Hickok would have been prepared for such an attack by taking a seat facing the door with his back to the wall, but a

Wild Bill Hickok – a daunting figure face to face, but as vulnerable as the next man to a bullet in the back of the head.

friend had jokingly refused to let him have his regular place, thereby giving McCall his chance. The killer was arrested, tried and, incredibly, acquitted. A retrial was ordered, however, and this time McCall was found guilty, and hanged in March 1877.

The nose have it, or if you have to be assassinated, it is always handy to have a couple of hundred surgeons around. In April 1926, the Italian dictator, Benito Mussolini, attended the opening ceremony of an international congress of surgeons. As the strains of the Fascist national anthem were struck up, Il Duce stopped in his tracks and snapped to attention. At that very moment a shot rang out. The assailant was Violet Gibson, a sixty-two-year-old Irishwoman who had come to Rome to shoot either Mussolini or the Pope. Mussolini turned out to be her would-be victim, but her success was limited. The

Mussolini sports a strip of sticking-plaster across his nose following the assassination attempt.

dictator's sudden movement had spoilt Violet's aim and, instead of blowing his head off, the point-blank shot had merely grazed Mussolini's nose. Scarcely extending the surgical repertoire of the congress, Mussolini was soon able to continue his official duties with a strip of sticking plaster across his nose to bear witness to the attempt on his life. As for Miss Gibson, she was magnanimously freed on her victim's orders, and deported.

Presidents are often assassinated, Kings are sometimes murdered, and Queens have been known to be beheaded, but the ultimate destiny of British Prime Ministers is a seat in the House of Lords. Not quite always so. At about 5 p.m. on 11 May 1812, the Right Honourable Spencer Perceval, Prime Minister of His Majesty's Government, was assassinated as he entered the House of Commons. A fairly colourless man in both character and deed,

A contemporary print of the shooting of Spencer Perceval.

Perceval's murder was not inspired by any controversial policy. The assailant, John Bellingham, was manifestly mentally disturbed, blaming the Government, and Perceval in particular, for his bankruptcy. He therefore exacted his revenge by firing a single pistol shot at point-blank range into the Prime Minister's chest, after which Bellingham sat down on a nearby bench and awaited capture. The assassin's evident mental disorder did not elicit any sympathy from the British legal system of the time, and he was tried, convicted and executed within the week.

Engelbert Dollfuss became Chancellor of Austria in 1932. It was a job few would have envied him, as the country was split between right- and left-wing groups who violently threatened to overthrow the government. Equally ominous was Hitler's rise to power across the border in

Chancellor Dollfuss after the SS got to him.

Germany, bringing with it the possibility of Austria's absorption into the Nazi Reich. Dollfuss managed precariously to hold on to power for two years until the Austrian Nazis, aided and abetted by Germany, made their attempt at a coup. On 25 July 1934, dressed in army uniforms, a group of Austrians who had enrolled in Himmler's SS stormed the Federal Chancellery in Vienna. In spite of warnings that an attack was imminent, scarcely any precautions had been taken by the security forces, and the SS men had little difficulty in finding Dollfuss and shooting him in the chest. The Chancellor was laid on a sofa from which he proceeded to engage his assassins in a restrained political discussion as he steadily bled to death. But as Dollfuss lay dying, the coup was coming to an end. Austrian police and army units belatedly arrived on the scene and arrested the murderers, who were subsequently executed. The affair had shown Hitler that the time was not yet ripe for the annexation of Austria, but he could afford to wait.

Sultan Abdul Hamid II warily surveys the crowd.

Sultan Abdul Hamid II was the ruler of the Ottoman Empire at the turn of the century. As the 'Spider's' empire crumbled into decay, his people grew more discontented and, not without some justification, he greatly feared assassination. One step taken to ease the Sultan's anxiety was a ban throughout the Ottoman lands of any public reference to regicide. The absurdity of this legislation was brought home in 1903 when the King and Queen of Serbia were murdered in a palace revolution. Although the royal couple, Alexander Obrenovic and his consort, Draga, had been shot and hacked to death, in the Ottoman Empire they were reported to have died of indigestion.

Victims of assassinations do not as a rule show a willingness to assist their would-be killers, but Rasputin was positively bad-mannered in the trouble to which he put his murderers. In December 1916 Rasputin was invited to the house of a 'friend'. There he was fed poisoned cakes and wine but, with the cyanide having little or no effect, he was then shot. The assassins left the 'body' only to find on their return that it had moved. So Rasputin was shot again, beaten with an iron bar, kicked, tied up and thrown into the River Neva. But the 'Mad Monk's' tribulations were not over – for he was still alive when they dumped him in the water. When the body was eventually fished out of the river by the authorities, an autopsy was carried out and revealed that the cause of death was drowning. A year later, the Bolsheviks dug up Rasputin's body from his grave and burnt it in what was supposedly a symbolic act, but, in the light of his previous stubborn refusal to die, perhaps the revolutionaries were simply not taking any chances.

An unusually clean and pious Rasputin before his grisly end.

Never the most popular of men, Rasputin was often threatened with assassination. Revolutionaries, reactionaries, spurned women and cuckolded husbands, all had their reasons for killing the 'Mad Monk'. One attempt that very nearly succeeded occurred in June 1914, when a deranged woman accosted Rasputin in the street and stabbed him in the stomach. Although Rasputin eventually recovered, the attack had far greater significance than anyone at first realised. At almost exactly the same time as Rasputin was stabbed, the Archduke Franz Ferdinand was shot at Sarajevo in an incident that was to spark off the First World War. There are reasonable grounds to speculate that, had Rasputin not been lying in a hospital recovering from his wounds, his presence at the Tsar's court might have prevented Russia's declaration of war. For Rasputin was an avowed pacificist, and on two earlier occasions when war had threatened, Tsar Nicholas had heeded his advice.

The violent death of a young man in a Deptford pub brawl could be a minor headline out of today's newspapers, but the homicide in question happened nearly four hundred years ago in May 1593. Furthermore, the dead man was no ordinary drunk but the celebrated Elizabethan playwright, Christopher Marlowe. Like his contemporary, Shakespeare, Marlowe, was a man of mystery. He certainly carried out espionage work for the government, and indications that he might have been 'turned' by the Queen's enemies make his violent end all the more intriguing. There has also been speculation that Marlowe was the victim of a homosexual *crime de passion*. The official verdict, endorsed by the coroner, was that Marlowe had become involved in a drunken fight with friends over some money and had been stabbed in the eye. However, a more sinister cast is given to the story by the revelation that Marlowe's 'friends' (who were granted free pardons for the killing) were employees of the Elizabethan spymaster,

Sir Francis Walsingham, who just also happened to have been the playwright's controller during his career as an agent.

There were so many attempt to assassinate Tsar Alexander II that he developed a reputation as a one-man disaster area. To be anywhere in his vicinity was felt to be so hazardous that the citizens of St Petersburg would not buy tickets for the opera unless they were given an assurance that the Tsar was *not* attending the performance. Finally, in March 1881, the assassins succeeded. A bomb was thrown at the Imperial cortège and exploded, injuring a child and a cossack guardsman but leaving the Tsar unharmed. Alexander ordered his carriage to stop and went to comfort the wounded man when a second bomb was flung. This time twenty spectators were killed and the Tsar was almost blown in half. He died about an hour later.

The aftermath of the first bomb. While chaos reigns, Alexander obligingly leaves his carriage and thereby helps the assassin to complete the job.

Blunders

In April 1918 Commander Ernest Boyce thought that he had pulled off a great coup. Boyce, the head of the British Secret Intelligence Service's operations in Russia, had acquired some vital documents that revealed the Bolsheviks' true relations with Germany. Admittedly Boyce had spent a small fortune in purchasing the papers, but they clearly proved that Lenin and Trotsky were German agents and that the Russian revolutionaries were in close contact with the German General Staff. The documents were passed on to two experts who promptly pronounced them fakes, pointing out that the papers, ostensibly a collection from sources throughout Russia, had all been typed on one machine. Staring failure and disgrace squarely in the face, Boyce did the only thing he could do. He sold the documents to the United States Mission in Petrograd for a sizeable profit

In 1879 a British army invaded Zululand and a base camp was set up at Isandhlwana, from which the expedition's commander set out to look for the main Zulu army. Unfortunately, while Lord Chelmsford was out looking for them, 20,000 Zulus found his camp. At first, the disciplined fire of the British infantry held off the massed attacks of the enemy. Soon, however, the riflemen began to run out of ammunition. Runners were sent from the firing line to fetch more cartridges, but even in the heat of battle bureaucracy reared its stubborn head. There were

The 'Thin Red Line' about to get thinner. Zulus close in on British troops at Isandhlwana.

ample stocks of ammunition, but many of the quartermasters refused to issue cartridges to men who were not from their own units. To make matters worse, the ammunition was packed in heavy wooden boxes, sealed by metal bands and with the lids held down by screws. Not only did they find that the screws were invariably rusted into the wood, but there were simply not enough screwdrivers. Valuable time was lost while the soldiers tried to prise open the boxes and get at their precious contents. Inevitably, the redcoats' fire slackened and the Zulus closed in. Without ammunition, it was a case of too few bayonets against too many assegais – barely 350 survived out of the British force of 1,800 men.

Two days after the declaration of war in 1939, Britain had still done virtually nothing to help her beleaguered ally, Poland. Many people felt that an early RAF air offensive on Germany was the best (and only) way in which Britain

The timid Sir Kingsley Wood stands next to the pugnacious Winston Churchill in a photograph of Neville Chamberlain's 1939 War Cabinet.

could affect the enemy's war effort. On 5 September, Leo Amery, MP called on Sir Kingsley Wood, the Air Minister, and suggested that the RAF launch an immediate air raid, using incendiary bombs, on the tinder-dry Black Forest. Both men knew that the region was full of German army munition dumps but, for Kingsley Wood, this was not sufficient excuse to destroy 'private property; the idea was shelved.

Napoleon's campaign in Germany and Austria during the autumn and early winter of 1805 is a testament to his military brilliance. This is not to say that the French Emperor was not ably assisted by the glaring inadequacies of his Russian and Austrian adversaries. At Austerlitz, Napoleon cleverly lured his opponents to attack him while he defended a strong position. The night before the battle, the Austrian general, Weyrother, in conference with his fellow commanders, outlined a long and complex plan that relied heavily upon the French conforming precisely to his predictions. As Weyrother spoke, the Russian commander, Kutusov, was fast asleep. Further problems occurred with the slowness of making a Russian translation of the Austrian battle plan. It was not until 3 a.m. on the morning of the battle that the orders began to be circulated throughout the army. The delay resulted in some of the Russian units failing to receive their instructions until after they were supposed to have moved. Thus the Austro-Russian army began the battle of Austerlitz in a state of ham-fisted confusion that was to end in total defeat and 26,000 casualties.

When the Armistice was signed in November 1918, the position of the German High Seas Fleet was decidedly unusual. It had avoided battle for most of the war, apart

The suicide of a fleet – the scuttling of the German High Seas Fleet.

from Jutland and a few brief clashes in the North Sea, and at the time of the surrender it was still an intact, immensely powerful naval force. The conditions of the ceasefire dictated that the fleet be interned until the peace treaty was negotiated. An odd situation developed with over seventy German warships at anchor in the British base at Scapa Flow, watched over by the guns of the Royal Navy. Tension increased as the diplomats failed to find a quick solution to end the war. The German commander, Admiral Ludwig von Reuter, deprived of information and a sitting target if war was resumed, made secret arrangements to scuttle his fleet. Isolated in the Orkneys, von Reuter relied to a great extent upon old newspapers for information on the progress at the peace talks. Finally, on Saturday, 21 June 1919, on the day when the original armistice agreement expired, von Reuter gave the order for the fleet to scuttle. Before the Royal Navy could intervene, the Germans had opened the sea-cocks and sunk the ships. It seems unlikely that von Reuter was aware that the armistice had been extended by two more

75

days, but it also seems certain that he had made a decision that the High Seas Fleet would never become a bargaining counter in the peace treaty.

By 1887 Morrell Mackenzie was recognised throughout Europe as one of the foremost specialists in the field of throat diseases. He had studied at London, Paris, Vienna and Budapest, and had written several learned works. It was little wonder, therefore, that Mackenzie's advice was sought in the treatment of Crown Prince Frederick of Prussia. German doctors had already diagnosed cancer of the throat and recommended the removal of the Prince's larynx. Mackenzie, however, saw things differently. To the delight of the Imperial court, the expert announced that the disease was not necessarily cancer and, even if it was, it was probably benign. He therefore felt that surgery was not required. In return for his services (and optimism), Mackenzie was knighted by his own country and decorated by Prussia with the Grand Cross of the Hohenzollern Order. But in November Mackenzie received some bad news from Germany; it was confirmed beyond doubt that Frederick had cancer. The news was not too good for the Crown Prince either. He had an operation in January 1888 but it was now too late to stop the spread of the disease. In March the Kaiser died and Frederick succeeded to the throne, but the new monarch, of whom so much had been expected, reigned for only 99 days before the cancer took its toll. Inevitably recriminations were unleashed with great abandon. The German medical fraternity was highly critical of Mackenzie's diagnosis, while he replied that they had transformed a benign growth into a malignant and terminal cancer. Mackenzie's career never fully recovered from his well-publicised error and he died four years after his patient. Europe was also to be the loser, for, as a result of Frederick's death, the new Kaiser was the young Wilhelm II, who proved to be as belligerent as his father had been moderate.

The Russo-Japanese War of 1904-5 was an unmitigated disaster for the Tsar's army and navy. The action took place in Manchuria, on Japan's doorstep but thousands of miles from Moscow and St Petersburg. It was not long before Russia's land and sea forces were bottled up in Port Arthur, leaving Nicholas II and his government smarting under this massive blow to their Imperial dignity. The situation needed a grand gesture; all that was offered, however, was farce. It was decided that a relief force be sent, and the Russian Baltic Fleet was chosen for the job. A glance at the map would have shown that the 18,000-mile voyage around the world was impractical, while it was common knowledge in the navy that the Baltic Fleet was badly led, badly equipped, badly trained and riddled with revolutionary agitators. Nevertheless, the Fleet set sail in October 1904. All the worst fears were soon realised when it entered the North Sea and sank some of the Hull fishing fleet, nearly precipitating war with Great Britain and certain annihilation by the guns of the Royal Navy. Fortunately, the incident was smoothed over and the

Mistaking Yorkshire trawlers for Japanese torpedo boats, the Russian Baltic Fleet scores several hits.

Russian armada sailed on around the continent of Africa. The fleet was off the coast of Madagascar when news reached it that Port Arthur had fallen to the Japanese. But, in keeping with the lunacy that surrounded the whole enterprise, they were ordered to proceed to the Pacific. Miraculously, they arrived off Korea by the end of May 1905 – only to be pounced upon by the Japanese navy at Tsushima. The Baltic Fleet had sailed around the world only to be slaughtered, their sole achievement being to make St Petersburg sue for peace.

General José Sanjurjo was a Spanish right-wing leader who went into exile in Portugal on the assumption of power by the Republican party. He should have stayed in his new home. Instead, he chose to organise a coup to overthrow the Spanish government. By 1932 his plans were laid and, understandably proud of them, it is reported that he confided his strategy to a prostitute during a moment of amorous respite. The details of the General's scheme were soon known in Madrid and the uprising was cancelled. Undismayed, Sanjurjo tried again in 1936, this time with closer security. A small aeroplane was prepared to fly him out of Portugal, but Spain's would-be saviour demanded that he be sartorially worthy of the occasion. Against the advice of his staff and the pilot, the aircraft was crammed full of the General's ceremonial uniforms. Not surprisingly, the aeroplane crashed on take-off, killing the fashion-conscious Sanjurjo.

General Sanjurjo during a period of imprisonment following one of his abortive coups d'état. The indignity of having to wear a convict's uniform must have been a sore tribulation for the fashion-conscious soldier.

Sex

One of the countless Allied plans to end the Second World War envisaged an air raid on Hitler's headquarters. At first glance, this does not seem a particularly original idea, except that this aerial bombardment was to consist of pornography, not high explosive. The American intelligence organisation, the Office of Strategic Services, employed a team of psychoanalysts who speculated that Hitler's psychological profile indicated that he might be an avid user of pornography. They therefore concluded that an inundation of lurid reading matter would either totally

Hitler shows Martin Bormann some new additions to his collection of 'artistic' photographs.

derange him or give him a heart attack. Huge stocks of pornographic material were collected and crates, designed to fly open on impact, were constructed. But the plan was finally abandoned due to 'shortage of aircraft' – or an attack of common sense on the part of the OSS's commanding officers.

Colonel Valentine Baker was one of Victorian England's finest cavalry officers. Commanding the famous 10th Hussars, he had introduced reforms in training and tactics that made him renowned and respected at home and abroad. Then, in 1875, he fell from grace. On 17 June a Miss Dickinson was seen clinging to the open door of a railway train as it sped between Walton and Esher. The train was stopped and the hysterical young woman said that she had been attacked by the man sitting opposite her in the compartment. That man was Valentine Baker. Amidst much public clamour, Colonel Baker was sent for trial on charges of assault with intent to ravage, indecent assault and common assault. Although it was basically just Miss Dickinson's word against the Colonel's, his claim that she took fright after misinterpreting a casual remark was rejected by the jury. He was sentenced to prison for twelve months, fined £500, and 'removed' from the Army. His career in England was ruined, but on his release Baker's undoubted military talents were not completely wasted, as he went on to serve with distinction in the Sultan of Turkey's army in the war against Russia and, later, as the commander of the Egyptian Gendarmerie. It is interesting to note that, in spite of his conviction, his old regiment and most of the military establishment retained a belief in his innocence. He was re-elected to the Army and Navy and Marlborough clubs, but his rehabilitation was never complete. A brilliant career had been ruined either by a moment's lust or a neurotic girl's imagination.

Colonel Valentine Baker in pensive mood at the time of his fateful train ride.

The Emperor Tiberius was fifty-six years old when he came to the throne. His life had been soured by violence and the need to repress his feelings, so that now, as absolute ruler of the Roman Empire, he indulged himself with abandon. As a bisexual, the range of his pleasures was vast, embracing a penchant for voyeurism and a partiality for oral sex performed by slave boys (his 'minnows') who swam with him in the baths. He made homsexual advances to temple attendants after a service and their refusal led to their legs being broken. He favoured the Isle of Capri as a hideaway from the cares of state, but it was not a happy place for those who annoyed him as they were simply flung over the nearest cliff.

One of the most famous homosexual scandals of the nineteenth century was the case of the Bishop and the Guardsman. The Right Reverend Percy Jocelyn, Bishop of Clogher, was the third son of the Earl of Roden, making him a pillar of both the ecclesiastical world and the nobility. On the night of 19 July 1822, he was in London and visited the White Hart Tavern in Westminster. During the course of the evening, the fifty-seven-year-old bachelor bishop was discovered performing a homosexual act with Private Moverley of the 1st Regiment of Guards. Reports stated that the bishop made every effort to escape but was hampered by the fact that he was not given the opportunity to pull up his breeches, which remained around his ankles. Finally conceding that resistance was useless, he surrendered to the constables but steadfastly declined to give his name – an understandable but short-lived attempt at anonymity. Bail was granted, and the bishop was released (he does not appear to have helped find Moverley's sureties). Not surprisingly, the bishop failed to show up for his trial, knowing that his career was ruined and that he faced the prospect of imprisonment. He fled to Scotland, assumed the name of Thomas Wilson, took a job as a butler, and died in poverty in Edinburgh in 1843. Less is known of the fate of Private Moverley, other than that the Duke of Wellington, aghast at the damage done to the prestige of the Church, Nobility and Army, threatened to deal severely with him. There is a third figure to add to the saga of the pederast clergyman. Eleven years before his tryst in the White Hart, the bishop was accused by a servant of having made an immoral proposition. In reply, Jocelyn, then Bishop of Ferns, brought the servant, James Byrne, to trail for libel. It was no contest. Byrne was found guilty and sentenced to a public flogging and two years' imprisonment. The ecclesiastical sodomite's subsequent fate may, therefore, be considered as just deserts.

The Empress Elizabeth, daughter of Peter the Great, certainly maintained the family tradition of sexual excess. Coming to the throne in her early thirties and free of the ties of marriage (unless there is any truth in the rumour that she married a Cossack peasant who sang in the Imperial chapel choir), she used her autocratic powers to ensure a constant sexual roundabout. Foreign ambassadors at the Imperial court reported that she abandoned herself to 'every excess of intemperance and lubricity' and noted that she had 'not an ounce of nun's flesh about her'. It would appear that a nun might have been the only piece of flesh that she did not make a grab for. It was not just the quantity of liaisons that marked Elizabeth's reign but also the variety. The Empress had a marked tendency towards transvestism. A feature of court balls became the requirement of courtiers to don the clothes of the opposite sex, while the Tsarina's favourite predilection was to wear the garb of a Dutch sailor (oddly enough, a disguise also used by her father).

The Empress Elizabeth refrains from her transvestite tendencies in favour of a voluminous gown.

Louis XIV of France was known as the 'Sun King', a title that reflected his brilliant court at Versailles. It would have been an equally fitting sobriquet if his brother, Philippe, Duke of Orleans, had been called the 'Sun Queen'. Presiding over a court of his own at St Cloud, Philippe indulged his own transvestite and homosexual tastes with a motley collection of lovers and hangers-on. One particular favourite, the Chevalier de Lorraine, was so dissolute that Louis was moved to send him into exile. But this was not before the Chevalier had been linked with the mysterious death of the Duchess of Orleans. An irony was that Philippe, known quite inappropriately as Monsieur, was a more than capable general. In fact, the ability in battle of this outrageously effeminate man made Louis so jealous

Philippe, Duc d'Orleans, appropriately depicted in flamboyant style as one of the Gods of Olympus.

that he deprived him of his military command. A cultured patron of the arts, twice married and the father of several children, Philippe was, to say the least, a man of many parts.

The Prince Regent, later to become King George IV, had a taste for the 'older woman'. It is a common enough fantasy among young men to want an older lover, while older men often have a preference for younger companions. George was not party to these common traits. He began by liking mature mistresses and the older he got, the older he liked them, with all his later paramours already being grandmothers by the time he took up with them. In 1819 he switched his affections from the sixty-three-years-old Marchioness of Hertford to the 'youthful' blandishments of Lady Conyngham, who was her predecessor's junior by sixteen years. But his change of 'mistress' was evidently not inspired by a desire for young blood, as it seems highly unlikely that Lady Conyngham was anything more than just a good friend.

Imperial Vienna with it waltzes, 'Blue Danube' and gay hussars was a lively place in the nineteenth century. The ruling Habsburg dynasty entered into the spirit of things even down to the usually timid Archduke Ferdinand Maximilian, whose speciality appears to have been a nice line in female impersonation. On one occasion, this royal drag artist had himself introduced at court as the Princess of Modena. On another occasion, dressed in a woman's nightdress, he treated the guards at the Schoenbrunn Palace to renditions from Bellini's *La Sonnambula* in the style of the famous soprano Jenny Lind, giving his performance from the Palace rooftops to an audience of highly amused soldiers.

The young Archduke Ferdinand Maximilian and the Schönbrunn Palace, the scene of one of his finest performances.

Like most of the Nazi hierarchy, Himmler was a mass of contradictions, leading a private life greatly at variance with his public utterings. While he preached the sanctity of wholesome Nazi ideals such as marital bliss, his own marriage was less than harmonious. He had married a divorcee (like several of his colleagues) who was eight years older than him. She provided him with money, respectability and a child, but he could find neither the time nor the inclination to settle into a normal married life. By 1940 he was having an affair with Hedwig Potthast, a young secretary on his staff, and soon afterwards began to lead something of a double life. His revised domestic situation was more than accepted by his fellow Party members, and he was 'lent' 80,000 marks by Martin Bormann out of official funds in order to set up his mistress in a love nest. They certainly needed the room, for Himmler was soon the proud father of two illegitimate children.

The not so happy couple – while Mrs Himmler seems content enough with married life, husband Heinrich appears to be less than pleased with the state of affairs.

After two years of the First World War, French morale had reached rock bottom. The bloodiest of the innumerable battles of 1916 was taking place around the vital fortress of Verdun, whose defence soon began to symbolise the entire French will to fight. A man of exceptional quality was needed to command the French forces: the man chosen was General Phillippe Pétain. The problem was that Pétain could not be found. Whilst armies fought to the death at the front, staff officers scoured Paris, seeking to inform the General of his momentous appointment. Mindful of Pétain's reputation as a ladies' man, they finally ran the white-haired, sixty-year-old to ground in the Hotel Terminus at the Gare du Nord, where he was happily ensconced with his mistress. The management initially denied that Pétain was a resident, but the staff officers found the General's boots (and a pair of lady's slippers) outside a bedroom door. Eventually

General Pétain, the victor of both the battlefield and the bedroom.

Pétain emerged and told the officer to find himself a room for the night; he would complete his current engagement and take up his appointment in the morning.

Ernst Röhm was one of Hitler's earliest followers in the Nazi movement and played a crucial part in the Führer's rise to power. So great was his importance that it counterbalanced the scandal of his well-publicised homosexual excesses. Röhm used his position as Chief of Staff of the SA – Hitler's brownshirts – to coerce young recruits into succumbing to his dubious charms. He used SA funds to procure boys, and sent his staff to act both as talent scouts and as guardians of his lovers' fidelity. Parties and orgies were held at SA headquarters whenever Röhm did not fancy venturing out to the famous homosexual haunts of Berlin's Turkish Baths, Kleist-Kasino and Silhouette club. Rohm's enjoyment of establishments such as these was all the greater because they had been denied him during a frustrating exile in Bolivia, spent serving in that country's army. In plaintive letters from South America he bemoaned the lack of his 'favourite form of activity' and requested sympathetic friends in Germany to send him pornography as a substitute for the real thing.

Emma Hamilton's place in history was assured by her affair with Admiral Nelson, but although he was by far her most famous lover, he was by no means the first. She arrived in London in 1779, aged about fifteen, and soon put her exceptional beauty to good use. She found employment at Dr Graham's 'Temple of Hymen', which was a cross between a brothel, strip joint and health club. Not surprisingly, she caught the eye of one of her clients, Sir Harry Fetherstonhaugh, and was subsequently established as his mistress in a love nest in the country. She

A satirical cartoon of an obese Lady Hamilton bemoaning Nelson's return to sea.

provided him with a child before transferring her affections to Charles Greville who, in turn, passed her on to his uncle, Sir William Hamilton. Although her senior by some thirty years, Hamilton married her and together they set up home in Naples where Sir William was the British Ambassador. They appear to have been relatively content until, in 1798, Nelson arrived on the scene. An affair soon blossomed between Lady Hamilton and the Admiral that was conducted with scant regard for social convention. This state of affairs was greatly facilitated by Sir William's naive faith in the 'purity' of their friendship, a faith that was to last until his death in 1803. But the social disapprobation that had been held in check during their affair was unleashed following Nelson's death at the Battle of Trafalgar in 1805. Emma became an extravagant and poverty-stricken outcast, the unwanted (and now grossly overweight) mistress of a dead hero. She was put in prison for debt and took to the bottle, before fleeing the country to avoid her creditors. She died a broken woman in Calais in 1815.

In spite of the number of sexual skeletons filling their own cupboards, Hitler and his cronies were never slow to use sex scandals as a means of disposing of their political opponents. No better example exists than the manner in which they gained effective control of the German Army. Generals von Blomberg and von Fritsch were respectively Minister of Defence and Commander-in-Chief of the Army during the mid-1930s, but by 1937 they were showing clear signs of opposition to Hitler's plans. Their removal was therefore deemed essential, but their rank and position precluded the Nazis' usual violent solution. However, von Blomberg to a certain extent dug his own grave by marrying his young secretary, about whom there were rumours of a shady past. A dossier on the bride was collected and passed around the Army and Nazi Party hierarchy. With the dissemination of the evidence that Frau von Blomberg had not only been a prostitute but had

General von Fritsch explains a point of tactics to Hitler, while General von Blomberg (centre) listens attentively.

modelled for pornographic photographs, the General was obliged to resign his post. Meanwhile, the Gestapo engineered a smear campaign against Von Fritsch, fabricating an extremely flimsy charge of homosexuality. Von Fritsch contested the accusation and, in a military court of honour, he was judged totally innocent of all charges. Nevertheless, Hitler still got what he wanted. The General's professional reputation was ruined, while he emerged an understandably disillusioned man. He resigned on 4 February 1938 (the same day as von Blomberg), and the path was clear for Hitler to win control of Germany's armed forces.

Prince Felix Youssoupoff gained world notoriety when, in 1916, he murdered Rasputin. But before that event he had achieved another sort of fame, but for entirely different reasons. Since his early teens Youssoupoff carried out a double-life as a transvestite. With a male companion he frequented the prostitute area of the Nevsky Prospect, dressed as a woman, finding pleasure in the propositions made by prospective clients. In later years he progressed to the nightclubs of St Petersburg and Paris, even claiming in his autobiography that he had flirted with King Edward VII (who, it must be stated, was ignorant of Youssoupoff's true gender).

Germany's Second Reich is remembered as a period of Prussian militarism embodied in the aggressively truculent figure of Kaiser Wilhelm II. But there was a softer, tenderer side to this era. Count Philipp zu Eulenburg and Hertefeld (the Kaiser's close friend) was the lover of General Count Kuno von Moltke (the military commander of Berlin). The monarchs of the German Empire were an equally amorous bunch, with the King of Württemburg in love with a mechanic, and the King of Bavaria smitten with a coachman. Although Paragraph 175 of the German Penal Code made homosexuality a crime that entailed a long sentence with hard labour, sodomy amongst the ruling class was so prevalent that it was known throughout Europe as the 'German Vice'. Even the élite Garde du Corps Regiment appeared on police files for mass fellatio orgies among its officers. Although there was no reason to accuse the Kaiser of homosexuality, it certainly pervaded his court, with his wife's private secretary and the Court Chamberlain in the ranks of those who indulged. One episode, never fully explained but amusing in its details, did involve Wilhelm II. At a party on the estate of Prince Maximilian Egon zu Fürstenberg, the Kaiser was entertained by a special cabaret. The star of the show was General Count Dietrich von Hulsen-Haeseler, the head of the military cabinet. Wearing a pink ballet skirt and a rose wreath, the General had scarcely finished his dance before he keeled over and died of a heart attack. Although he had honourably passed away in the service of the Kaiser, it was

The Kaiser and his military entourage plan the evening's pas de deux.

only belatedly decided to dress him in his uniform, by which time rigor mortis had set in. The military supremo who had died, not with his boots on but with a pair of dancing pumps, almost suffered the indignity of going to Valhalla wearing a tutu.

On 16 February 1899 the President of France, Felix Fauré, suffered a heart attack at the Elysée Palace. A sad but none too startling fate for a fifty-nine-year-old man, burdened down by the affairs of state. The interesting fact about Fauré's death is that, at the time of being struck down, his burden consisted of his naked young mistress. After a meeting with the Prince of Monaco, Fauré had repaired to his rooms for an 'interview' with Jeanne-Marguerite Steinheil. Several hours later neither had emerged and it was only when servants heard screams that they entered the love-nest. They found the President in a 'significant state of undress', unconscious, yet gripping the hair of his naked, hysterical girlfriend. With typicallly Gallic understanding of such a delicate situation, the palace officials cut Madame Steinheil's hair and she was bundled off home, leaving the President to die three hours later in rather more dignified circumstances. Madame Steinheil's adventures did not end at the Elysée Palace. Nine years later she was tried for and acquitted of the murder of her husband and mother, and then tried her hand at running a boarding house in South London. She subsequently married into the British aristocracy, and died in 1954 aged eighty-five.

The genetic blemishes of the Habsburg dynasty have, of late, overshadowed many assessments of its history. One very good reason for this is the occasional first-rate eccentric thrown up by the family that ruled vast areas of

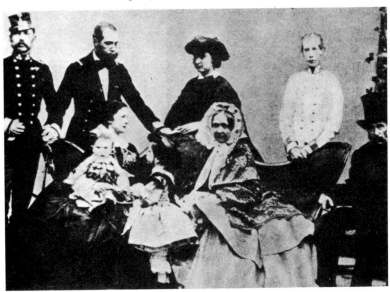

The Habsburg family with the black sheep, Archduke Ludwig Viktor, standing second from the right.

Europe before the First World War. The Archduke Ludwig Viktor, whilst not insane, was certainly rather odd. As the youngest brother of the Emperor Franz Joseph, his official duties were comparatively few and therefore he spent much of his time indulging his homosexual proclivities, being known to the court as 'Lutzi-Wutzi', which form of endearment was soon being employed by his Viennese masseur. There were limits even to Habsburg misbehaviour, however, and, after a messy episode in a Turkish bath with a butcher's boy, Ludwig was sent to live in Klessheim Castle, near Salzburg. Inspired not so much by an attempt to rehabilitate him but rather by a desire to remove temptation, only female servants were employed at the castle.

It is no wonder that Charles II was known as the 'Merry Monarch'. The names of at least thirteen of his mistresses are known to historians, while it is extremely likely that there were many others whose services were rendered either casually or secretly so that their names are not known. The lovers that have been identified are a tribute to Charles's catholic taste in women, who ranged from the English aristocracy (Lady Byron) and the French nobility (Duchess of Châtillon) to London actresses (Nell Gwynne). There also exists a degree of uncertainty about the number of his illegitimate children, but a fair indication of their number is that six of his bastard sons were created Dukes. In spite of his reputation as a lover, Charles's marriage was childless, and his relationship with his wife was a thing of duty and politeness rather than an affair of passion.

In the 1980s the world is used to the controversy over artificial insemination, but in the 1930s it was not a

97

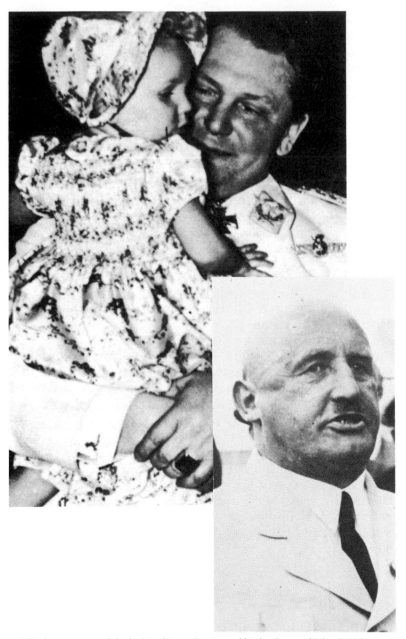

The doting parent and the doubting bigot – Goering and his daughter, and Julius Streicher.

popular topic of conversation. It was certainly far from popular with Hermann Goering, who was on the receiving end of a smear campaign launched by his political rival, Julius Streicher. It was claimed that Goering's baby daughter was the product of artificial insemination – an accusation so ludicrous that Streicher was obliged to retract it. But then, Streicher was not noted for his rationality. A Nazi from the earliest days of the Party, he edited a semi-pornographic newspaper that was rabidly anti-Semitic. The classic degenerate, Streicher was without a redeeming feature, being sadistic, corrupt and totally unscrupulous. Were it not for his obvious insanity, he might have wrought even greater evil, but in 1940 Goering got his own back and supervised an enquiry that resulted in Streicher's dismissal from all Party posts. Ironically, five years later the two men were to stand together in the same dock at Nuremberg. While Goering cheated the hangman, Streicher, the lunatic to the last, believed he was the victim of a Jewish conspiracy, his final words being 'Heil Hitler!' shouted from the scaffold.

Failures

In December 1852 Louis Napoleon, the nephew of
Napoleon Bonaparte, was proclaimed Napoleon III,
Emperor of France. There had never been a Napoleon II
(Napoleon's son and heir had died in 1832 merely bearing
the title of Duke of Reichstadt) and there very nearly
failed to be a Napoleon III. Twice, in 1836 and 1840,
Louis Napoleon had made inept attempts to seize power.
The first took place early one October morning when the
would-be emperor introduced himself to the 4th Artillery
Regiment at Strasbourg, calling on them to follow him.

NAPOLEON III.

*Napoleon III, whose success with his moustaches was not matched by his early efforts to seize
power.*

Unfortunately, the soldiers were none too impressed. Nor was King Louis-Philippe who had Louis Napoleon arrested and deported to America. The next few years were spent planning another coup that was finally 'unleashed' in August 1840. Together with fifty of his followers, Louis Napoleon landed at Boulogne and offered himself to France as its leader. The French authorities. response was to arrest him. This time, he was put on trial and sentenced to life imprisonment. But Louis Napoleon had more luck in getting out of France than getting into it and, in 1846, he escaped, disguised as a builder's labourer. There seemed to be no way in which he could win the throne of his uncle. It was his tactics that were at fault though, rather than his unsuitability, and a new approach brought great dividends. He was elected President in 1848 and, with the power of the ballot box behind him, it was only a short step to becoming Emperor.

It had always been one of the first duties of a monarch to secure the dynasty by producing a number of suitable heirs. The consequence of this was that any infertile king or queen was classed as a failure, and knew themselves to be such. Perhaps the most prolific but unlucky breeder was Queen Anne, who spent most of her married life in a state of pregnancy. She had married Prince George of Denmark in 1683 and together they ensured that Anne was pregnant every year until 1700. But in spite of their sterling efforts, none of their children survived. Besides twelve miscarriages, one child was stillborn and five others died at an early age of dropsy. It is ironic that the most fecund of the Stuarts should have been the last, her failure to produce an heir resulting in the arrival of the Hanoverian dynasty on the throne.

Perhaps it is a little harsh to include Friedrich von Paulus in a list of failures for, although he was commander of the defeated German forces at Stalingrad, he was never completely in control of all command decisions. His army, the Sixth, was caught in the Stalingrad pocket but Hitler refused to allow him to retreat. Instead, von Paulus fought on, his postion becoming more untenable as his army was savaged by the Russian winter and the attacks of the Red Army. Finally, on 31 January 1943, after sustaining over 200,000 casualties, von Paulus surrendered the remaining few thousand men of his command. His decision earned him the scorn and anger of the Fuehrer and helped make him the propaganda tool of his Russian captors. Von Paulus's war was not to end until 1953, when he was finally released from a Russian prison and faced with the difficult task of settling down to life in Communist East Germany.

Von Paulus at the surrender of Stalingrad.

Publius Helvetius Pertinax followed the Emperor Commodus as ruler of the Roman Empire. It was not a popular
decision – with Pertinax. He was chosen by the soldiers to
be their Emperor but he did not want the job and tried to
foist the 'honour' off on several other members of the
Senate. Pertinax's reluctance was well-founded, for less
than three months later he was killed by the very soldiers
who had chosen him. There then followed what can only
be described as the sale of the millennium when the palace
guards put the Empire up for auction. The winning bid
came from Marcus Didius Julianus, who offered 6,200
denarii to each of the Praetorian Guards. It seems that the
only person who did not realise that the whole affair was a
farce was the new Emperor. The people of Rome pelted
him with stones whenever he left the palace and there
were soon armies marching from the provinces to depose
him. It did not take too long before even Julianus saw
which way the wind was blowing. At first he tried to buy
off the rebels, then, in desperation, he fortified his palace
against attack. Little more than two months after making
his purchase, Julianus had lost his throne, becoming the
victim of yet another assassination by the Imperial
bodyguard. He had scarcely got value for money.

Fate sometimes makes people born failures; everything
they touch turns to stone. One such unfortunate was
James Edward Stuart, the son of King James II. Because
his father was unpopular and few wanted to have him as
an heir to the throne, rumours were circulated that the
King's son had been smuggled into the royal maternity
room in a bedwarming pan, replacing the Queen's
stillborn child. A slur that he was an impostor surrounded
him thereafter, providing an inauspicious start to a career
that was to become a catalogue of failure. Six months after

his son's birth, James II was deposed, and father and son went into exile in France. For the rest of his life, James Edward made a series of ill-timed, half-hearted attempts to win back the crown of England. In 1708 he caught measles just before his followers launched an invasion on his behalf, and the sickly leader of the rebellion merely sailed around the British Isles without landing. A better-organised effort in 1715 might have brought more success, but James Edward's lack of leadership and weak character contributed to the rebellion's defeat. After spending six weeks in his homeland he resumed his exile. Even his private life was a disaster, for, although his wife provided him with two sons, their marriage was such that she was moved to take the extreme step of spending two years in a convent away from her husband. It was with much relief that James Edward Stuart handed over the irksome task of saving the Jacobite cause to his son, 'Bonnie Prince Charlie'. Now, out of the limelight, 'the King across the water' spent the rest of his life in Rome; a dull, devout and dreary failure to his end in 1766.

In the eighteenth century Britain's most powerful weapon was the naval blockade. The Royal Navy waited outside enemy ports (usually French), preventing ships and commerce from entering or leaving. That, at least, was the theory and it usually worked well enough. But during the war against Revolutionary France, the blockade of Brest was so ineffective as to be almost non-existent. The naval force under Lord Bridport was so poorly positioned that the French lugger, *Rebecca*, which sailed out of the port with every intention of surrendering to the first Royal Navy ship it found, ended up spending a fruitless three days searching for one. This was not an example of Gallic cowardice but a wily attempt to plant false information on the British. The plan belatedly succeeded when the lugger was finally boarded and the 'captured' documents sent to the Admiralty.

However extensive his training and however deep his experience, the undercover agent is always liable to falter under the unbearable strain put on a man's nerves by a life of constant tension. During the last war, General Delestraint, an officer appointed by de Gaulle to lead the French Resistance's Secret Army, was travelling through occupied Paris. It had been arranged that he spend the night at a safe house, and the General was pleasantly surprised when an attractive woman answered his knock at the door. His delight, however, rapidly turned to despair when he realised that he had completely forgotten the password. Both he and the woman knew the rules and, after a few minutes' idle chat, he was obliged to leave without entering the apartment, instead having to take a room at a nearby hotel. But now the agent's night turned from a nuisance into a disaster; in his flustered state, he signed the register with his real name and, as a result, was arrested early next day. His night of mental chaos was to cost him his life: he was taken to Germany and died in Dachau concentration camp.

The very fact that 'John Brown's body lies a-mould'ring in the grave' can be directly attributed to his complete misjudgement of the prospects for a mass slave rebellion. He had been an effective, if violent, anti-slavery activist in Kansas and Missouri, freeing Negroes and leading raids on the camps of pro-slavery groups. But on 16 October 1859 he attempted a coup that was insanely ambitious. At the head of an 'Army of Liberation' that numbered less than two dozen men, he planned to seize the US Government's arsenal and armoury at Harpers Ferry, Virginia, and thereby secure the weapons for a mass slave insurrection throughout the southern states. Making his move at night, he captured the arsenal buildings relatively

105

John Brown – whose fame owes more to his martyrdom than to his blundering efforts to promote a slave uprising.

easily, but his hopes for an instant army of Negro freedom fighters were soon dashed. His invitation to rebel was met by a negative response that was almost total, while the authorities' reaction was quick and effective. By the time Government troops arrived on the scene, only five of Brown's 'army' remained uninjured, and it took a mere three minutes for the last flickering embers of resistance to be extinguished. Brown was duly tried and found guilty of murder, treason and conspiring with slaves to rebel. As a flamboyant martyr, Brown greatly assisted the cause of abolition, but he also deserves to be remembered as a singularly naive and inept mastermind behind a fiasco of a rebellion.

Sometimes history's failures do not have to make their own mistakes, their misfortune stemming rather from the behaviour of others. This was certainly the case in the sad tale of Lieutenant Jaheel Brenton Carey but, unfortunately, he also appears to have done everything in his power to deepen the hole into which he had been pushed. In 1879, Eugène, the French Prince Imperial and son of the late Emperor Napoleon III, pulled strings at Queen Victoria's court to be allowed to join the campaign against the Zulus in South Africa. Finally permission was granted, but on the understanding that the VIP was to be kept away from the fighting. This was easier said than done, for the Prince was an energetic young man in whose veins ran the blood of the great Napoleon. Sometimes he was allowed to join scouting patrols and it was on one such occasion that his party of nine men was ambushed by Zulus. Amongst those killed was the Prince Imperial and amongst those who survived was the patrol's commander, Lieutenant Carey. An enquiry found that Carey was guilty of misbehaviour in the face of the enemy; in truth, his fault lay in not dying with his royal charge. Many understood that Carey had been made the scapegoat, but instead of biding his time and taking considered steps to achieve his rehabilitation,

The ill-fated Prince Imperial.

he mounted a clumsy public campaign and took to pestering the Prince's mother, the Empress Eugènie. So great a nuisance did the lieutenant become that Eugènie released to the press some letters that had come into her possession, in which Carey admitted his feelings of fear and panic during the ambush. Carey's subsequent military career offers a sad postscript to the tragic incident. He was sent to Coventry by his fellow officers, who turned their backs on him in the mess and curtailed any conversation that he tried to join . Obstinately (or bravely) Carey endured this life for another six years, before dying in Bombay, a broken man.

General George Armstrong Custer's place in history derives from his disastrous command of the US 7th Cavalry at the Battle of the Little Big Horn in 1876. But an intimation of 'Long Hair's' notable lack of military talent

General Custer – whose confident body language belied his failures in the schoolroom and the battlefield.

came very early in his career when, in 1861, he graduated from West Point Military Academy, recording an inauspicious 34th place out of a class of thirty-four.

Drink and Drugs

The assassination of President Abraham Lincoln in April 1865 created a huge empty space in American politics. It fell to his Vice-President, Andrew Johnson, to attempt the impossible task of filling the gap and stepping into the great man's shoes. But the task soon proved too much for him. Already unpopular with many of Washington's politicians, Johnson eased the immense pressure on himself by a steady intake of alcohol. The most traumatic experience looked certain to be his inauguration, so he fortified himself with medicinal whisky and, as a result,

President Johnson, who appears either intent on looking resolute, or is merely trying hard to focus.

111

faced the ceremony in a state of alcoholic equanimity (albeit with notably slurred speech). His inability to speak coherently, to remember the oath of office, or to walk in a straight line, were later explained as the effects of a recent 'illness'.

In November 1885 the British Empire took another step forward when it deposed King Theebaw of Burma and annexed his kingdom. The action had been precipitated by Theebaw's misrule, his interference with the teak trade, and his flirtation with French economic interests. The task facing the British expeditionary force was not too daunting, and it was made all the easier by Theebaw's inveterate drinking. They had been able to monitor the situation, and chose the right moment to make their move thanks to a series of telegrams from Rangoon that always began: 'King still drinking.'

British troops tell King Theebaw that he is drinking after hours – using this as an excuse to depose him.

The real Calamity Jane was nothing like the freckled, singing and dancing tomboy portrayed by Doris Day in the musical film of the Wild West's most famous cowgirl. Virtually the only concession towards feminity displayed by Jane in real life was a rumour that she was, at one time, Wild Bill Hickok's lover. Apart from that one exception, she spent most of her time proving that she could outshoot, outfight and outdrink any male master of these dubious activities. Her later years saw her health ruined by drink and, in spite of several attempts to help her, she became a liability to her friends. Money raised in a benefit to provide for her old age was spent on a mammoth alcoholic binge, and a job at the Pan-American Exposition did not survive a bar-room brawl and her assault on two policemen. She lived up to her name right to the end and, in 1902, only a year before her death, she is reported to have shot up a bar in Montana.

Calamity Jane enjoys a beer with a friend.

Drinking habits have changed over the centuries. The eighteenth century was perhaps the most bibulous, but by the time of the Napoleonic Wars attitudes were beginning to change. Both Napoleon and his adversary, the Duke of Wellington, were considered by their contemporaries to be very moderate drinkers. But what appeared to be a small amount in the 1800s is today the intake of someone with a drink problem. Observers wrote that Wellington only had four or five glasses of wine at dinner and about a pint of claret afterwards. Napoleon was remarkable for drinking even less, taking a mere half-pint of claret with each meal and even cutting this down to a couple of glasses of watered wine when in exile on St Helena.

Albert Edward, Prince of Wales, later King Edward VII, was a famous connoisseur of wine, food and women. Of the three pursuits, drink was perhaps the least essential, and the Prince dispensed with long drinking sessions after meals in favour of a quick glass of brandy and the ladies' company. Nevertheless, Edward usually ensured that he had ample supplies to slake his thirst. He was certainly well prepared for a trip on the River Nile in 1868, accompanied by some twenty guests. Provisions for the party on their six-week cruise included 3,000 bottles of champagne, 4,000 bottles of claret, cases of sherry, beer and liqueurs, and 20,000 bottles of soda water. This reservoir of liquid sustenance filled an entire supply boat, but doubtless helped to make the Sphinx even more enigmatic than usual.

The Prince and Princess of Wales with some of their fellow travellers in Egypt.

It was said of the Roman Emperor Maximinius Thrax that he liked a glass of wine. In fact, he is reported to have drunk a jug every day. But what seems on the surface to have been a fairly normal intake becomes something quite remarkable when it is noted that the jug in question was a Capitoline amphora which held forty-six pints of wine. Roman historians wrote that at times of stress Maximinius drank himself into a stupor – one cannot, however, help being rather surprised that anything gave him cause for concern, given his daily consumption of nearly six gallons of wine.

The image projected by Nazi Germany was of a master race of supermen, pure in thought, word and deed. But

115

Robert Ley sweeps another unsuspecting fräulein *off her feet.*

even a brief examination of the lives of the Nazi leaders shows how far they were from attaining the Teutonic ideal. Amongst these tarnished heroes was Robert Ley, head of the German Labour Front, who was given the disrespectful but appropriate nickname 'Reich Boozer'. He announced to the German people, 'Any man may smoke and drink as much as he can tolerate, as long as it does not harm his body and hamper his work.' Privately, Ley maintained a state of near total inebriation. The stories of his drunkenness and subsequent outrageous behaviour were common knowledge and even a source of amusement to the usually puritanical Hitler. One often-repeated anecdote told of a dinner party at Ley's house when the host, inflamed by drink, stripped his wife in order proudly to display her physique to his embarrassed guests. Ley's exuberance ultimately proved to much for his spouse and she committed suicide. Consoled by the bottle, however, the widower survived his bereavement and had notched up four marriages by the time he killed himself in 1945.

The American writer Edgar Allan Poe easily qualifies for a place in virtually every section of this book. He was a failure both as a university student and a military cadet, being thrown out of the University of Virginia (after only one term) for bad gambling debts, and dismissed from West Point (after a year) because of his 'gross neglect of duty'. He was frequently ill and given to bouts of insanity that were characterised by violent outbursts, leading to a suspicion that he had committed a murder in 1841. His sex life was also colourful, including, amongst other aberrations, a marriage to his 14-year-old cousin. But, above all, his life and death were dominated by his dependence on drink and drugs. He ended his days in 1849, having been found semi-conscious in a Baltimore saloon. Sadly his last words, 'Lord help my poor soul,' were scarcely worthy of his previously outstanding performance in all other categories.

Edgar Allan Poe seeks the reassuring touch of his hip-flask.

In spite of her later puritanical image, in her youth Queen Victoria was by no means teetotal. Although beer 'did not agree with her' and champagne made her 'giddy', she was most partial to sweet ale and negus, a beverage similar to sweet mulled wine. But as her weight soared to nearly nine stones, the diminutive Queen (she was barely five feet tall) determined to diet and cut down on her boozing.

One of the most famous drug addicts of the twentieth century was Hermann Goering, Hitler's flamboyant heir apparent. In 1923 he was badly wounded during the abortive 'Beer Hall' uprising and was given morphine to ease the pain. This treatment soon turned into a dependence on the drug, which was fuelled by his

Sick and addicted to drugs, by the end of the Second World War Goering's physical condition had reached rock-bottom.

depression at the coup's failure and his enforced exile from Germany. Finally, in September 1925 Goering was admitted to an asylum in Sweden (his wife's native country) and was obliged to undergo a six-month cure for his addiction.

Anti-Nazi propaganda certainly made use of Goering's drug addiction and it is therefore difficult fully to assess whether he really managed to kick the habit. Albert Speer intriguingly recalled a story that Goering had been sued for 'improperly administering morphine' to a woman in a night club whose dress had caught fire. Goering had injected her with morphine to relieve the pain of her burns, but his 'patient' subsequently took him to court in order to gain compensation for the needle scar. Less fanciful, however, are the reports that Goering developed an addiction to paracodeine, but, although he was observed munching pills as if they were sweets, it seems likely that they contained only a very small drug dosage.

The notorious gunfighter Clay Allison had more than his fair share of shoot-outs, being credited with fifteen killings, but, apart from the odd bullet wound, he emerged relatively unscathed. It was therefore rather ironic that he should die in a freakish accident. One night, after a long drinking bout in town, he set off back to his ranch, barely capable of driving his buckboard. Somewhere on the trail he fell off his seat. The gunslinger died as the rear wheels of the carriage broke his neck.

Throughout history, the rewards of a successful siege have been rape, pillage and looting for the victorious soldiery. But in September 1857, when Delhi was captured from the Indian mutineers, the first priority for the conquering British troops was drink. An officer wrote that theft came

The British Army launches an assault on the gates of Delhi, inspired by a desire to get to grips with the mutineers (and the city's stores of liquor).

a very poor second to the quest for beer, wine or brandy as the soldiers fought their way through the city streets. Even pursuit of the mutineers slackened as the troops spent most of their time reeling from one looted shop or cellar to the next. Finally, in desperation, one of the army commanders ordered that the city's liquor stores should be destroyed because the drunkenness of his men was seriously delaying complete victory over the rebels. It was to take several days before all Indian resistance was overcome and the British forces (some no doubt nursing a hangover) set about the serious business of looting the city.

Deaths

On 12 August 1822 Lord Castlereagh, Foreign Secretary and Leader of the House of Commons, cut his throat with a penknife that he had bought from a street trader for a shilling. It was widely known that Castlereagh had been under a great deal of stress for a considerable period of time, and was showing signs of what we now recognise as a nervous breakdown. But it was not merely affairs of state that drove the Foreign Secretary to suicide. It has come to light that Castlereagh was the victim of a blackmail plot which, together with the burdens of government, made

Lord Castlereagh in his finery, before the crisis that ruined his life.

him kill himself. It transpires that Castlereagh occasionally enjoyed the company of prostitutes whom he picked up on his way home to St James's Square from the Houses of Parliament. One day in 1819 he was propositioned. He accepted and accompanied the whore to a nearby room. It was a set-up. Once in the bedroom, the prostitute revealed 'herself' to be a boy wearing women's clothing and, simultaneously, 'witnesses' rushed in. The gang threatened to denounce him as a homosexual (a punishable crime as well as a social stigma) unless he gave them money. For the next three years one of the most powerful men in Britain was the victim of continuous harassment by a gang of London crooks. For Castlereagh the only escape was death.

King John of England was a gourmand in an age when large appetites were common. But John's love of food and drink was ultimately to prove his undoing. As his kingdom collapsed into war and chaos, John grew fatter and fatter. Great pains were taken to ensure that the finest wines were always available at each stop on the royal tour and, at a time when all good Catholics refrained from eating meat on Fridays, John ate beef every day, hoping that gifts for the poor would excuse this infraction of ecclesiastical rules. In October 1216 John finally reaped the fruits of his over-indulgence by dying at Newark after a short illness. The source of his malady had been given as a surfeit of either peaches or lamphries (eel-like fish) washed down with too much new cider.

On 19 May 1536 Queen Anne Boleyn was executed at the Tower of London. She had been found guilty of a variety of trumped-up charges (including incest, adultery and conspiracy to poison), but her real crime had been a failure to provide Henry VIII with a male heir. The law provided that she be either burnt or beheaded at the King's pleasure, but Anne requested that, instead of the English custom of using an axe, she be executed in the French style, with a sword, and Henry acceded to this bizarre preference. England, however, was not exactly full of trained swordsmen queuing up to carry out the job, and the execution was therefore postponed for twenty-four hours to allow a professional from Calais to arrive. This executioner was obviously worth waiting for, because his two-handed sword severed the Queen's head with one blow.

Perhaps the most famous death of the Third Reich was the murder of the twenty-three-year-old Horst Wessel. Bringing the full weight of the Nazi propaganda machine to bear, Joseph Goebbels made Wessel into the

Horst Wessel on the cover of the sheet music for his marching song 'Die Fahne hoch'.

movement's most famous martyr. A nondescript poem, written by Wessel, was set to music and became the official marching song of the Party, while its author posthumously came to embody the finest ideals of Nazi manhood. Needless to say, the legend was almost entirely a fabrication. In fact, Wessel was a down-and-out, failed student who had joined the Nazi Party in 1926 and later enrolled in the SA. He steadily became disenchanted with the movement and resigned from his 'Brownshirt' unit so that he could spend more time with his prostitute mistress. Nevertheless, in February 1930, Wessel became involved in a fight with a gang of left-wing activists and was shot by Ali Hohler. It is, however, in question whether Wessel died defending his Nazi beliefs, for it seems likely that Hohler, the former pimp of Wessel's lover, was motivated by something more basic than political ideology.

The image of Hitler presented to his doting female followers was of a man whose only love was the Fatherland. However, he certainly felt amorous stirrings of a more tangible nature towards Geli Raubal, the daughter of his half-sister. But the relationship between the neurotic Fuehrer and the naive young girl was doomed to failure, since the middle-aged man became both jealous and stiflingly protective towards his niece. In part this may be explained by the conflicting emotions of attraction to Geli and his otherwise paternal role in her life. Cloistered together (with Geli's mother) in Hitler's Munich apartment, their arguments grew ever more frequent and heated. Finally, in September 1931, while Hitler was en route to a political meeting in Hamburg, Geli shot herself. Inevitably there were many rumours of blackmail and murder, but there is no doubt that her death left Hitler inconsolable and with an emotional scar that was further to disfigure his already suspect psyche.

Fifty years before the birth of Christ, Rome was enjoying one of those golden eras that broke through the mire of palace revolutions, decadence and violence. Three of Rome's most able sons formed a triumvirate: Gnaeus Pompeius, Gaius Julius Caesar, and Marcus Licinius Crassus. Of the three, Crassus was the least talented but, as the richest man in Rome, he was an essential part of any government. He suppressed Spartacus's revolt, but his attempt to emulate his colleagues' victories on the field of battle failed abysmally. While Pompey and Caesar met success in nearly every engagement, Crassus's army was soundly defeated by the Parthians at the battle of Carrhae and its general captured. His execution was a gruesome, if apt, end to a capitalist trying to be a soldier; his Parthian captors poured molten gold down his throat.

'Gone but not forgotten' – Queen Victoria gazes wistfully at a bust of Prince Albert, Princess Alexandra watches the birdie, and the Prince of Wales just looks fed up with the whole business.

Perhaps the most famous death of the nineteenth century was the demise of Prince Albert of Saxe-Coburg-Gotha, the husband of Queen Victoria. The Prince Consort died in December 1861 after a month's illness; his wife's mourning was to last rather longer – forty years. The cause of Albert's death was typhoid fever contracted at Windsor Castle, where the drainage and sanitation system had been little improved since the Middle Ages. However, Queen Victoria had other ideas about how her husband had succumbed. She believed that Albert had died of worry and grief over the revelation that the Prince of Wales had taken a mistress while serving with the Army in Ireland.

Like those of a great many violent men, Al Capone's end was singularly uneventful. The Chicago gang leader had been diagnosed as suffering from syphilis when he entered prison in 1931. Although he received treatment, it proved impossible to arrest the advance of the disease and, by the beginning of 1947, the neurosyphilis had resulted in substantial brain damage. On 19 January he suffered a brain haemorrhage when at his Florida estate. Bronchial pneumonia set in, and six days later 'Scarface' died in the bosom of his loving family, aged forty-eight.

They first realised that something was wrong when Stalin did not ring for his dinner to be brought to him. But so great was the fear inspired by the Soviet ruler that his guards were frightened to go in and see what had happened. In order to evade his wrath, they sent an old maid into his room to check on him, but even when she reported that the great man was lying unconscious on the floor, they were still uncertain about what action to take. Finally, after much debate, a party of high-ranking

Joseph Stalin – a man who trusted no one (and that clearly included the photographer).

Praesidium officials agreed to accept the responsibility, and Stalin was, at last, examined by doctors. They diagnosed a brain haemorrhage caused by cerebral arteriosclerosis and high blood pressure, and confided that his chances of survival were slim. They were right. On 5 March 1953, 'Uncle Joe', the murderer of millions, passed away.

Richard the Lionheart was not the man that popular history would have us believe. In recent years his chivalric crown has slipped somewhat as historians have pinpointed his violence, greed, homosexuality and poor kingship (he was only in England for two short periods during a ten-year reign). But at least he played the part of the hero when fatally wounded at the siege of Chaluz. An arrow struck him in the shoulder and, although at first his condition was not serious, the wound became gangrenous.

It is recorded that as his death approached, the King ordered that the archer who had fired the arrow (and who was now a prisoner) be brought to him. Magnanimously, Richard gave his killer a free pardon and a gift of money before he finally expired on 6 April 1199. If that was the end of the 'Lionheart', it was soon the end of the archer, for Richard's men did not obey his orders. He was taken to the dead King's sister, who instructed that the unfortunate be mutilated, flayed and torn apart by horses.

Of all the Nazi leaders captured at the end of the war and put up for trial at Nuremberg, Hermann Goering probably made the most determined defence. It was as if his latter years of fading influence in the Reich were now all behind him and a new era had dawned. If he believed this, his dream was soon shattered. Slimmer, fitter and receiving treatment for his drug addiction, Goering assumed the leadership of his fellow prisoners and fought a skilful, if hopeless, defence against the Allied prosecutors. Inevitably he was found guilty and sentenced to death, but two hours before he was to hang, on 15 October 1946 (more than a year after the war in Europe had ended), he took poison. Cheated of exacting justice, it is believed that the court added its own postscript by having Goering's ashes thrown into the last remaining incinerator at Dachau.

Henry V is remembered as a paragon of medieval valour, immortalised in Shakespeare's play. The bard concludes his story with Henry showing himself to be as adept at wooing his bride as he had been at beating the French army at Agincourt. Perhaps it is as well that Shakespeare finished the tale there, for Henry's death ill-befitted his heroic image as the warrior king. He died in 1422, not in battle, nor even in England, but at Vincennes, near Paris, a victim of the ignoble disease of dysentery. It was a singularly inappropriate and premature end for a monarch who, it has been said, held the leadership of all Christendom within his grasp. In fact, even as the thirty-five-year-old sovereign lay dying, he was making plans to lead a new crusade to the Holy Land.

One day in October 1920, King Alexander of Greece took his dog for a walk in the grounds of his palace at Tatoi, near Athens. The King was a tragic figure who had been coerced into taking his father's place on the throne but whose wife was denied the rank and privileges of a queen. During the course of their melancholy promenade, the King's dog became involved in a fight with the pet monkey of the vineyard keeper. Alexander tried to separate the two animals, but for his pains was bitten in the ankle by the

Alexander, the luckless King of Greece, and his pet dog, Fritz, who was directly responsible for the King's undoing.

monkey. His injury did not appear too serious and, after the wound was dressed, he walked back to the palace. Two days later, however, blood poisoning set in, and shortly afterwards the king died – a fatal victim of kindness to animals.

In the genealogical tree of England's monarchs, some six hundred years and a William separate William the Conqueror and William III, but they have something in common other than their Christian name: they both died after suffering what appeared to be a minor riding accident. In 1087 William I attacked the French town of Mantes. Riding through the streets after its capture, his horse stumbled and the king was violently thrown against the pommel of his saddle. He was carried in agony to a nearby priory, where he languished in pain for most of the summer until his internal injuries resulted in his death on 7 September. Although just as active a soldier as the Conqueror, William III's accident happened during a recreational ride near Hampton Court. He was thrown from his horse after it stumbled on a mole hill and in the fall broke his collar bone. From this apparently insignificant injury, complications set in and, on 8 March 1702, the king joined his namesake as another fatal victim of horseplay.

Violence

One unpleasant refinement of the gangster wars during America's prohibition era was developed by Messrs Scalise and Anselmi, formerly of Sicily but, at that time, residents of Chicago. Their contribution to the cause of blood and mayhem was to perfect a technique of rubbing garlic onto their bullets, thereby supposedly enhancing the chances of a gangrenous infection developing in their victims' wounds. Such subtleties as garlic were, however, markedly absent when the two hoodlums were themselves called to account. On 8 May 1929, that well-known sports fan Al Capone conducted some baseball-batting practice on Scalise's and Anselmi's heads.

One of the likeliest candidates for the title of most unpleasant Nazi was Hermann Esser who, in spite of his nefarious deeds and high position in the Reich, was never brought to trial at Nuremberg. Even Hitler called Esser a scoundrel and 'a conceited coward' (the latter comment referred to the convenient 'illness' Esser contracted at the time of the Munich Putsch and which kept him in bed throughout the uprising). Rabidly anti-semitic and extremely violent, Esser's domestic life was, if anything, even more frenetic. He boasted openly that he lived off his girlfriends and, on one notable occasion, relied on his mistress to warn his wife that he had contracted venereal disease from yet another woman. With the Nazi seizure of power, Esser was allowed to focus his limited intellect on

Hermann Esser, whose bank clerk's features belied his cruel and violent nature.

major issues and, in 1933, he became a highly unlikely Minister of Economics for Bavaria. It is hardly surprising that Esser's period in office began with an act of revenge rather than reform. On the night of his election victory, he summoned Dr Stützl, the former Minister of the Interior, to his office and proceeded to pour boiling water over his feet (the unfortunate Stützl recovered from this ordeal but a year later was trampled to death by members of the SS). In fact it was Esser's rank unpleasantness that was ultimately to prove his salvation, for he was soon categorised as manifestly unsuitable for any responsible position, and slipped down the Nazi hierarchy. But whatever else, Esser was a survivor. He came through the post-war de-Nazification process and lived until the early 1980s.

The Emperor Marcus Aurelius, a sensible, deep-thinking

ruler, was succeeded by his son, Commodus. Nicknamed the 'Monster', Commodus was a sexual psychopath and sadist who ruled as if he was trying to compensate for the sanity of his father's reign. An early intimation of his character came when, aged twelve, he ordered that a slave be thrown into the palace furnace because the Imperial bath water was too hot. As Emperor, however, the scale of his cruelty and sexual excess was increased, with 300 boys and 300 girls press-ganged into his bi-sexual harem. When he tired of sexual frolics, Commodus turned to violence, dressing cripples as snakes and then using them as archery targets.

Richard I is usually credited with being a soldier of great chivalry who honoured and respected his Moslem adversaries, the Saracens. However, the 'Lionheart' was not above butchering over 2,000 Arab prisoners that he had captured after the fall of Acre to the Crusader army in July 1191. He did not kill the captives immediately, but had them slaughtered a month later, after negotiations with Saladin, the Saracen leader, had broken down.

The Indian Mutiny of 1857 was notable for the appalling atrocities committed by both sides, each inflamed by the stimulants of religion, fear and drink. The most infamous deed of the war was the massacre at Cawnpore, when European women and children, held captive after the men had been slaughtered, were themselves murdered. The mutineers had taken fright at the approach of a British relief force and, in their panic, had hacked to death some 300 prisoners, disposing of their bodies in the river or down a well. They scarcely made any effort to hide the massacre and, after Cawnpore's recapture, the British troops were incensed by the scenes of carnage that met

British soldiers at the scene of the massacre at Cawnpore after its recapture.

their eyes. Thereafter, few mutineers were taken prisoner, save for those whose lives were spared only to allow for punishment before death. Brigadier-General Neill ordered that captured mutineers were to be taken to the scene of the massacre where they were forced to lick clean a square foot of the room's blood-stained floor. When this task was completed, usually with the encouragement of the lash, the miscreants were taken out and hanged.

No one was safe from Ivan the Terrible. His enemy, Prince Andrew Shuisky, probably expected a violent death, but must have wished for a less unpleasant fate than the one that befell him; being eaten alive by Ivan's hunting dogs. Nor was it wise to be the bringer of bad news to the Tsar's court. On one occasion, a messenger had his foot transfixed to the floor while he made his report and, when he had finished, he was led off to be tortured. Similarly, in

Ivan the Terrible.

a rather extreme breach of diplomatic etiquette, Ivan ordered a French envoy's hat to by nailed to his head. It was not much fun being a Russian courtier either, for Ivan had a habit of personally impaling any hanger-on who annoyed him. To complete the picture, it was even a tricky business being Ivan's friend. His favourite, Prince Ivan Viscovaty, fell from royal grace and, as a consequence, was hung upside down and sliced to death. But this did not satisfy the Tsar who, together with his son, went to Viscovaty's palace and raped his widow, whilst the Tsarevitch, clearly a chip off the old block, forced his attentions on the Prince's daughter. Even the arts suffered under Ivan's dubious patronage when he ordered the architects Barna and Postnik to build a new church in Moscow. He was delighted with their work, but his pleasure was such that he became obsessed with preventing a duplicate of the church, St Basil the Blessed. Ivan therefore solved the problem and rewarded the architects by cutting out their tongues, chopping off their arms and putting out their eyes.

History remembers Napoleon as a genius and one of the world's truly great men. But it is often overlooked that no one could have achieved his triumphs without a certain degree of ruthlessness. In 1798 he launched an over-ambitious and ill-fated expedition in the Middle East, which clearly showed up the hard side of his character. After the city of Jaffa surrendered to his army, Napoleon found himself unable to feed the Turkish garrison that he now held prisoner. His solution to the problem was to have the 2,000 men massacred.

The Wars of the Roses raged virtually unchecked from 1455 to 1485. Ostensibly, it was a struggle for the throne of England fought out between two rival noble families, York and Lancaster, but men swopped sides as their sentiments and the tide of war dictated. The upshot of this protracted conflict was that the English medieval aristocracy was all but wiped out. So violent was the age that death could come from any direction – even from a comrade-in-arms. At the battle of Tewkesbury in 1471, the Lancastrian army was defeated. As the Yorkists launched their final charge, the Duke of Somerset rode up to his fellow Lancastrian, Lord Wenlock. Instead of commiserating, he declared that Wenlock had failed to help him in the battle and, with a single blow of his battle-axe, he split the nobleman's head in two. But Somerset did not long outlive his victim – he was captured by the Yorkists and beheaded a couple of days later.

In the early thirteenth century, Pope Innocent III preached a crusade against a heretical movement in south-west France. Known as the Albigensian Crusade, the conflict was (like most religious wars) notable for its cruelty and fanaticism. In July 1209 the crusaders attacked the town of Béziers where there were known to be many heretics. At the moment of victory, the Papal Legate, Arnold Amalric, was reminded that many loyal Catholics were numbered amongst the town's 7,000 inhabitants. His reply was typical of the age: 'Kill all! Kill all, for God will know his own.' The population of Béziers was thereupon massacred, many of them being slaughtered in a church where they had sought sanctuary.